The Traveler's Guide to Life

A Memoir of Freedom, Connection, and Discovery

By

Zhara York

Little Wild Experiences: A Journey of Risk, Culture, and Self-Discovery

by Zhara Michelle York

© Zhara Michelle York, 2025

First Edition: 2025

Published by Little Wild Experiences Press

For inquiries, contact: info@littlewildexperiences.com

Disclaimer

To protect the privacy of individuals, the author has changed names. The events described are based on real experiences and are intended for storytelling purposes only.

Dedication

To the dreamers who wander, and to those who dare to begin. To the souls I met along the road — the ones who passed me by and the ones who stayed — you are all part of my story.

*To my mother, **Azaira G. Sanchez**, whose love and spirit still guide me, and to my stepmother, **Rosa E. Velásquez**, who showed me what true family means — two women of resilience and true power, each in their own way.*

*And to my father, **Miguel B. Fernández**, who taught me that music is a language of its own. Though we were never truly close, I admire him as a musician and honor him for bringing into my life the two remarkable women who shaped the best parts of me.*

Acknowledgments

This journey has never been mine alone. To my family and friends who encouraged me when I needed it most — your love has been my anchor. To the strangers who offered me a couch, a meal, a story, or simply laughter in the middle of nowhere — you turned miles into memories.

To my closest friends: thank you for inspiring so many of these stories. Without your presence, your laughter, and the magic of our connections, these adventures would not have carried the same joy. You reminded me that travel is not just about places but about people — the conversations, the inside jokes, and the shared chaos that made every moment unforgettable.

And finally, to myself — for having the courage to keep going, to keep believing, to keep writing. This book is as much a celebration of resilience as it is of wanderlust.

Table of Contents

Introduction

"A mind that is stretched by a new experience can never go back to its old dimensions." – Oliver Wendell Holmes

Traveling has never just been a hobby for me—it's been a lifeline. A pulse. A rhythm that flows through my days and makes life feel rich, textured, and alive. While some chase stability, I've always been drawn to motion. There's something magical about the world unfolding before you—the rush of unfamiliar streets, the laughter of a language you barely understand, the quiet sense of belonging in places you've never been.

I didn't start traveling just to escape the mundane—though yes, like many, I've felt that urge. For me, it started as a genuine curiosity : How do other people live? What makes them tick? What do they eat, celebrate, fear, and hope for? That curiosity evolved into something deeper: a way to understand myself.

Every journey I've taken has reflected something back to me— something I needed to learn, something I needed to face. Travel reminds me that I'm okay. That I'm capable. That I can pick up and go, and still feel whole, even when everything around me is foreign.

To me, travel is the most honest path to personal growth. It strips away comforts and routines, forcing you to meet yourself wherever you are. You get to see the world, yes—but more importantly, you get to see yourself in it. That's where the transformation begins.

It's not about the places themselves as much as about who I become through them: the confidence that grows from navigating airports alone, the empathy that expands by living inside another culture, the strength I discover when things don't go as planned. These are the reasons I keep moving.

This book is not a guide to destinations. It's not about the trips themselves as much as it is about the becoming that travel inspires. It's about what travel has taught me about myself: resilience, openness, courage, and joy.

So, these pages aren't a catalog of adventures. They are a reflection of what it means to grow when the only compass you have is your own.

I always wanted to write—about my life, but in a more storytelling way. I believe that if we knew more about others, we could better identify with their situations, making our own lives more comforting by helping us move forward and answering the questions that hold us back. When we know someone else out there has gone through the same thing and has done what many fear to do, we get to open our wings with freedom and no hesitation.

My aim for this book is not only to teach you, to help you move forward, and to make you laugh, but also to help you find yourself.

Chapter 1
Where Boldness Begins

Sometimes life calls for change. And not just the kind that rearranges your schedule or nudges you into a new job, but the kind that flips everything upside down, shakes the dust off, and throws you into the unknown. That's where I found myself. It wasn't just a matter of needing a new job—I needed a new world entirely. I wanted to move somewhere that would challenge me to grow, somewhere that would demand reinvention. A place where nobody knew my name, where I knew no one, and where everything around me was foreign. I craved a total reset. And what better place than China?

I had never been there. My home, my familiar surroundings, my comfort zone—everything I'd known—was thousands of miles away. I've always had a streak of boldness in me, a sense of adventure that pushes me to leap before I overthink. So I made the decision: China it is.

People often assume that getting a job overseas is complicated. It's really not. At least, it wasn't back then. Especially for Westerners who spoke English—or even just spoke it fluently enough—there was an abundance of teaching opportunities. Nowadays, many countries require English teachers to hold a certificate in teaching English as a second language. But when I took the leap, it was simpler. China had more flexible requirements, making it one of the easiest countries to start teaching—even if you didn't have a teaching degree or extensive experience. That may sound questionable from an educational standpoint, but for someone trying to get their foot in the door, it was an opportunity. One that could open more doors later on, even if teaching didn't end up being my long-term path.

At that time in my life, I had just finished a four-year degree in criminology. I know that probably sounds like a strange turn—going from criminology to teaching English in China. But when you're fresh out of school and the world expects you to have "experience" you couldn't possibly have yet, you do what you can. I was in my mid twenties, on my own, with no financial safety net. No friends or family nearby to lean on. I needed a full-time job, but more than that, I needed to start building my life.

So when I saw an ad posted in my university's English Language Department for teaching positions in Beijing, something clicked. I was going through a lot emotionally—maybe too much to unpack here— but I just knew I had to leave. Beijing became my target, my escape, my new beginning.

I didn't have much holding me back. I had finished school. I had a roommate but no real ties. No partner. No obligations. I had no idea what was waiting for me on the other side of the world. But I did know it was the perfect time to leap into something new. I've always believed that the more time you spend hesitating, the more likely you are to miss out on the very thing that might change your life.

China became my first real overseas living experience as an adult. I had moved before, but this was different: this time, I was moving to work, and

I wasn't planning on returning anytime soon. With just a couple of suitcases and no idea what the future held, I boarded a plane to a country I had never seen. It was scary. But it was also thrilling. And I've never regretted it.

I made friends. I learned Chinese—enough to get by, at least. But to be honest, I didn't connect deeply with the culture. That's not to say I had anything against it; it just wasn't for me. I've always believed that language and culture go hand in hand. If you don't fully embrace one, the other becomes difficult to master. Still, I adapted. I learned to survive in an environment completely different from everything I knew.

I discovered that you don't need anything around you to feel at home—you only need yourself. You make a place home by being there, by showing up, by owning your journey. That realization alone made the entire experience worth it.

So here's what I learned: If you don't like where you are, move. If you're tired of the same drink, try a new one. Be bold. Take risks. Try new foods. Shake things up. Because life is too short to stay stuck—and the world is too big not to explore.

As Ralph Waldo Emerson said, *"Do not follow where the path may lead. Go instead where there is no path and leave a trail."*

And that's exactly what I did.

Chapter 2
When a Trip
Becomes a Turning Point

There are many stories I could share, each with its own spark of magic, chaos, or surprise—but this one stands out. Maybe because it wasn't just a trip; it became the spark of a life-altering decision. At that moment in my life, I needed to change everything. I was emotionally drained, overwhelmed, and, as usual, itching for a shift. I've always had this tendency to shake things up when life feels too still. Some people call it impulsive. I call it survival.

It was a totally random decision—go to Dubai. And yes, I chose to go in the summer. Who does that? Apparently, me. The plan was simple: two weeks, just enough to hit pause, clear my head, and get back to New York in time for work. But deep down, this trip wasn't just a vacation. I was running from the mess, hoping a change in geography might also change something inside me.

Before landing, I already had a few tours booked through Airbnb. I always do that—not just for the experience but because it's the easiest way to meet people as a solo traveler. Strangers become adventure buddies, even if just for a few hours. I visited the desert, hung out with camels, and did the whole "Dubai checklist" thing. I even met a girl on the plane—she was also traveling solo. We exchanged numbers and planned to meet later in the city.

And let me just say, Dubai was a culture shock. When I went, it was already modern and impressive, but it has since changed rapidly—and continues to evolve. Now things are different. The rules are still in place, but there's more flexibility. At the time, it felt a little complicated to navigate, but looking back, I'd say not so much. Nowadays, you can legally purchase bottles by registering your foreign passport online as a tourist or by getting a simple alcohol license if you live there. But back then, none of that was easily accessible or clearly explained.

Everything I experienced happened during a very particular moment, when the city was still transitioning into what it is today. I had read that alcohol could be hard to find, and it was true. You could buy drinks, but only in bars that were part of hotels. The friend I met on the plane bought a couple of wine bottles on arrival. I didn't. I figured I'd just go out if I wanted a drink—no big deal. But later, I would seriously regret not grabbing one at the airport.

Once I landed, I checked into my Airbnb. It was a shared apartment, and I remember it clearly. I had to show ID to the building concierge before heading up. There were supposed to be three roommates—a girl I never met, and two guys. One of the guys was out of town (he was the one renting me the room), and the other one, my host, greeted me. He seemed cool. That night, I really wanted a glass of wine. And of course, I had none.

My host casually offered to help. "I know someone," he said. And just like that, I found myself involved in what felt like a black-market wine transaction. He made a call, we waited about an hour, and then he got a phone call. "He's downstairs." My host went to meet the guy, handed over the money, and returned with the bottle. It was honestly hilarious—like we had just done something terribly illegal, all for a bottle of wine.

A few days in, the guy who originally rented the apartment messaged me to say his roommate was throwing a little get-together at a friend's place and that I was welcome to join. Everyone I met there was super welcoming, trying to make me feel at home. There was even a DJ spinning house music. It was such a vibe. I remember thinking: Wow, I could live here. But vacations have a way of fooling you into believing that a city is something it might not be. Still, no regrets—I eventually did move to Dubai, but that's another chapter.

The next morning, I had a desert tour scheduled—my second one. The first had been a standard day trip: dune bashing, motorbiking, Arabic food, belly dancing, fire shows—all that touristy goodness. This second one was different. It was overnight. I had always wanted to spend the night in the desert, and this was my chance.

I was picked up midday. There was one other guest in the car, a quiet woman. The driver tried breaking the ice, and slowly, we all started talking. It felt strange that it was just the two of us, but I didn't ask questions. Later, I learned she actually worked for the tour company and was only there to accompany me so I wouldn't feel alone. Kind gesture, I thought.

That night in the desert was everything. The dunes whispered in the wind, and the stars blanketed the sky. If I could do it again, I'd bring wine. I love wine. Sitting under the stars with a glass would've been perfection. But apparently, for overnight stays, alcohol had to be arranged ahead of time. I missed that memo.

We were transferred from one camp to another by camel—at night. That ride was magical. The desert under moonlight, the silence, the slow sway of the camel—it was surreal. We stayed up late, talking until sunrise, the wind carrying our conversation across the sand. In the morning, we were greeted with breakfast before being driven back.

Back at the Airbnb, I rested for a bit and then texted the girl from the tour to meet up. She knew the city better than I did and had offered to show me around. We agreed on a meeting point. Dubai in the summer is no joke. The five-minute walk to the train station felt like a marathon under a blow dryer. Once inside, the AC felt like heaven. But the minute I got off the train? Oven again.

She arrived late—ten minutes of sunburn later—and took me to a local market where I wanted to buy a belly-dancer outfit. The haggling was intense. I hate bargaining, but thankfully, she did all the talking. After scoring the outfit, she stopped by a spice shop, and we struck up a conversation with the vendor. He was charismatic and funny. We exchanged numbers and took a picture with him. It was spontaneous and completely delightful.

We grabbed some food and decided to keep exploring. I wanted to see Burj Al Arab. Of course, we couldn't go in—you need a reservation or to be a guest—but I wanted a photo. Afterward, we figured, why not hit the beach?

Bad idea.

The beach in Dubai during summer is like sitting in a hot tub that's trying to kill you. But I was curious, so we went. It took two trains and two buses to get there. During one of the bus rides, it was absolute madness—people packed in like sardines. I started laughing out loud; it was so ridiculous. A guy next to us joined in, and before we knew it, we were all talking. Turns out, he had just moved to Dubai looking for work. Somehow, we invited him to the beach. So now, I was headed therewith two people I barely knew—one from the desert, one from the bus.

We took pictures, shared lunch, and laughed like old friends. It was bizarre, but I loved every second. When I think about it now, yes, it was a little crazy. But those moments are the ones that stick.

After I got back home, I stayed in touch with all of them. I even met up with the girl from the plane again in New York. The girl from the tour? We reconnected when I eventually moved to Dubai. That trip wasn't just about sand dunes and heatwaves. It led me to the decision to leave the U.S. again—for the second time—and make Dubai my home for a while.

To me, traveling isn't about luxury resorts or fancy restaurants. It's about connection. It's about blending in, talking to strangers, riding crowded buses, eating local food, and living like a local. That's the way I do it. That's the way it sticks.

"A journey of a thousand miles begins with a single step." – **Lao Tzu**

Chapter 3
A Foreign Land, A Familiar Leap

Moving across the world had never sounded unreasonable to me. In fact, it felt like the only logical choice when everything around me was falling apart. After finishing my undergraduate degree, I was emotionally drained. My mother had just passed away, and too many things were unraveling at once. Grief, stress, uncertainty—they weighed on me like a stone. And instead of waiting for life to fix itself, I did what I always do when things fall apart: I moved.

I had heard from some classmates that teaching English abroad was a good option after graduation, so I started searching online. The listings were endless, but only one caught my eye. The salary was fair, and the cost of living in the country was low. China wasn't a place I had ever pictured myself living, but that job posting turned out to be the catalyst for one of the most life-defining decisions I've ever made.

After a few back-and-forth emails with someone from HR, I had my interview. It felt easy—fluid, like I was meant to be part of this new chapter. A few days later, I received an offer letter. I was thrilled. It was official. I was moving to Beijing.

I was completely new to this—new to finding international work, new to visas, new to the nuances of relocating to Asia. HR instructed me to apply for a business visa, which felt odd at the time since I was going to be teaching. I didn't question it much—I just wanted everything processed and my flight booked.

What I didn't know then was that this first job, while not ideal, would open many doors later. At that moment, it didn't have to be perfect. It just had to be the next step.

The journey to Beijing was exhausting—over 19 hours of travel, including a layover in Canada. I remember being woken up repeatedly for airplane meals on that long leg from Vancouver to China. By the time we landed, I was floating in a mix of excitement and disbelief. I had done it. I was in China. I had moved with nothing but two suitcases and a blurry sense of what came next.

I walked through the terminal dazed, heading toward baggage claim, still processing the magnitude of the move. One suitcase came through. The other didn't. Just my luck. I reported it missing and realized with a sharp pang that this wasn't just luggage—it had a small container of my mom's ashes. That crushed me. I stood at the airline's lost items counter for over an hour trying to explain everything. By the time the report was filed, I had missed my school pick-up.

To top it off, I had no way to call anyone. My phone didn't work, and I hadn't thought to set up international service before I left. Yes, I know—it was a rookie mistake. I eventually used a payphone to call the school and update them. Then I found a cab.

I gave the driver the address. He nodded—apparently, he knew where to go. But halfway there, I realized something else was missing: my debit card. I must've left it in the payphone. This wasn't just any card; it was my lifeline. I had no cash and very limited access to money. So I asked the driver to turn around.

He didn't speak English. I didn't speak Mandarin. I flailed around with a translator app, broken body language, and exaggerated gestures until he understood. We returned to the airport. But of course, the card was gone. Defeated, I asked him to drive me to the hotel anyway.

Checking in was a whole new challenge. The staff didn't speak English either. I relied again on gestures, poor Wi-Fi, and the translator app. Eventually, I got my room key and flopped onto the bed. But I wasn't done. I still needed to call the bank to cancel my lost card—and then figure out how to get a new one sent to China, even though they could only ship it to my registered New York address. So I had to send them a secure message online with a new address... and of course, the hotel's Wi-Fi was barely functional. It took forever to do anything.

At this point, all I could think about was getting a drink. A simple glass of wine to ease the tension. But it turns out that's not so simple in Beijing. I ventured outside to find a bar—or anything resembling one. I had no local currency, so I used my credit card to get cash at an ATM, despite the outrageous fees.

Eventually, I spotted a building that looked promising. Music was playing, and a doorman stood at the entrance. Maybe it was a lounge. I walked up and tried to ask for a drink—again, with gestures. The man smiled and waved me downstairs. I followed, thinking finally. At the bottom, I was handed a microphone.

A karaoke bar.

Clearly, they thought I had come alone to sing. I must have looked ridiculous acting out the gesture of drinking—apparently, it looked more like singing. I laughed awkwardly and left.

Still determined, I wandered into a convenience store. The labels were all in Chinese characters, the shelves stacked with unfamiliar spirits. I grabbed what I thought was vodka and returned to the hotel. I poured a little into a disposable cup and took a sip.

It wasn't vodka.

It was Baijiu—an intense Chinese liquor made from fermented grains. One sip, and I spit it out instantly. I couldn't do it. I gave up on the drink and surrendered to my jet lag. The night was restless. I barely slept, and by the time I woke, it was nearly noon. I was starving.

I stepped out again to find food. I wandered until I found a local restaurant. No English menu, no familiar smells. The waiter handed me a menu entirely in Chinese, but thankfully, it had pictures. I pointed to what looked like a fish soup.

What arrived at my table was a whole fish, staring back at me, floating in a deep red broth. I took one sip.

My mouth went numb.

The spice, which I later learned was probably Sichuan pepper, lit up my lips and tongue like fire. I motioned for water, only to be handed a steaming cup of hot water, which is common in China. Not ideal when your mouth feels like it's burning.

I paid and left.

As I walked down the street defeated again, I saw something that looked like salvation: McDonald's. And yes, I went in. I didn't care. I needed something familiar. I probably ate more McDonald's in that first month in China than I had in the previous five years.

I knew right then that this was going to be a very different life.

But despite everything—the mistakes, the language barriers, the logistical chaos—this was my path. I had chosen it. And somewhere in the middle of cultural confusion and lost luggage, I was discovering something else: I could do hard things. I could face the unknown and figure it out.

It's funny how the discomfort of a new place mirrors the discomfort of emotional healing. Both hurt. Both stretch you. And both eventually shape you into someone stronger.

I had taken the first step into the unfamiliar—and somehow, that felt more like home than anything I had known in a long time.

Chapter 4
The Holiday That Found Me

There are certain holidays that leave a mark on your soul—not because of where you are, but because of who you're with—or, in some cases, because of who you're missing. Christmas has always been one of my favorite times of the year. The energy, the warmth, the traditions—it all meant something to me. So when I moved to Dubai, I quickly realized how different things would be.

The United Arab Emirates is a Muslim country, and naturally, Christmas isn't a traditional celebration. While Dubai is incredibly modern and has adapted to international tourism, at the time I lived there, things were still transitioning. You could see some Christmas decorations in malls—trees, tinsel, a few cheerful ornaments—but it wasn't the same. It wasn't home.

I had friends in Dubai, yes. But the closest ones were Muslim, and while they were lovely and respectful, Christmas didn't hold the same emotional value for them. And the acquaintances I did have who celebrated it weren't close enough to share something as personal as the holidays with. I needed something more—something familiar, something warm, something like home. That's when I remembered my friend in Thailand.

He traveled there every year around the holidays, and by some miracle, he happened to be there at the time. When I called and asked if I could join him and his family for Christmas, he welcomed me with open arms. It felt like the universe gave me exactly what I needed.

I booked my flight and headed to Pattaya, where his apartment and family were. This wasn't my first trip to Thailand—in fact, it's the country I've visited the most. Every time I go, I find something new to fall in love with. This time, it gave me the holiday I was so desperately missing.

A driver picked me up from the airport and took me on the two-hour journey from Bangkok to Pattaya. It's amazing how quickly the scenery shifts—from city skyscrapers to open green fields and small towns. I love that drive. It eases you into the slower, more grounded pace of life outside the city.

My friend and his family greeted me with such warmth. We talked, laughed, and shared stories—it felt like a tiny piece of New York had found me halfway across the world. He suggested a trip to Chom Thong, near Doi Inthanon—the tallest mountain in Thailand—and I immediately said yes.

We stayed at the Parinda Garden Resort, a serene place surrounded by bungalows, gardens, and the kind of stillness that makes you stop and breathe. The resort was simple, peaceful, and perfect. Breakfast was included, the staff was kind, and it felt like the kind of place that brings you back to yourself.

The journey up the mountain was as beautiful as the destination. Winding roads, thick greenery, and that unmistakable scent of nature— Thailand has a way of gently grabbing your heart without warning. We had lunches and dinners in local spots, nothing fancy, just places that served fresh food under simple canopies beside rivers. I remember one dinner vividly—a massive grilled fish, steamed vegetables, and drinks, all for less than $30 for three people. In places like this, luxury isn't measured by expense but by authenticity.

One afternoon, we visited a Thai spa in Op Luang National Park —the kind with hot springs, wooden lodges, and massages surrounded by trees. It wasn't fancy or staged for Instagram. It was real. The water was hot, the steam natural, the setting untouched. I remember paying something like $10 for the entire experience. That's the magic of Thailand—you don't need much to feel like you have everything.

On the road back to Pattaya, we stopped at a cozy little café surrounded by more trees than I could count. I even got a haircut and blow-dry for $5 before flying back. It sounds like such a small detail, but in moments like that, you realize how far simplicity can go in making you feel human again.

I've been to Thailand many times, and it never disappoints. If you ever find yourself wandering the streets of Pattaya, don't miss Nong Nooch Tropical Garden, where you can watch elephant shows or even hold a tiger cub, like I did. There's also Khao Chi Chan, where a massive Buddha is carved into a mountainside, standing 358 feet tall. And then there's Walking Street—wild, loud, electric. During the day, it's calm. At night, it becomes a world of its own.

But what mattered most on that trip wasn't the sightseeing, the food, or the spas. It was the feeling of belonging—of being seen and understood during a time when I felt far from everything I knew. That Christmas didn't look like the ones I was used to, but it became one of the most special holidays I've ever experienced.

Sometimes, home isn't a place. It's a moment, a feeling, a person who reminds you that you're not alone.

"In some ways, we are traveling in time now. We just happen to be prisoners of the present in the eternal transition from the past to the future." —Neil deGrasse Tyson

This story is dedicated to my dear friend and his family—my unexpected Christmas angels. You know who you are.

Chapter 5
Trapped in HongKong

During my time living abroad, one of the most tedious but unavoidable steps everyone faces is obtaining a proper working visa. Each country has its own complex process, and China is no exception. Back then, if you wanted to transfer your tourist visa to a working visa, you had to make a quick trip to Hong Kong. At least, that's how it worked in those days.

My employer told me I'd need to go to Hong Kong for the visa transfer. What was supposed to be a short, simple trip—just a few days—turned into something very different.

Hong Kong is a fascinating place with a layered, almost theatrical history. It once belonged to the United Kingdom, then to Japan, then back to the UK, and finally, in 1997, it became part of the People's Republic of China. Still, Hong Kong has its own government and economic system. It's not a province of mainland China but a *Special Administrative Region (SAR)*, much like Macau, which once belonged to Portugal.

Here's where it gets confusing: when you leave mainland China for Hong Kong, you're technically leaving the country, even though Hong Kong *belongs* to China. It's like stepping into a parallel universe with a different currency, language, and legal system—while still under the same flag.

This bureaucratic magic trick would later trap me in one of the most unexpected travel stories of my life.

The Beginning of a Bureaucratic Adventure

While living in China, I had recently changed jobs. My new employer was responsible for assisting me with all the paperwork to obtain my working permit. They introduced me to an outsourced agency to handle the visa process, and after signing my contract, I started communicating with them.

It was about a month before the Chinese New Year—February, the time when everything slows down because government offices close for the holidays. The agency advised me to make my trip to Hong Kong before the break. After a visit to the immigration office in Beijing, I was told I had to go to the Chinese embassy in Hong Kong to finalize the process. Once I got my working visa stamped there, I could return to Beijing and have my work permit issued.

I found the process strange but didn't question it. It was, after all, the only legal route to keep my job.

A Smooth Start (or So I Thought)

With the Chinese New Year approaching, the timing actually seemed convenient. I could get my visa sorted and then spend a couple of extra days exploring Hong Kong. My coworker helped me book everything—a train to Shenzhen (right next to Hong Kong) and a flight back to Beijing. The plan was to stay in Shenzhen, since hotels there were far cheaper, and cross into Hong Kong by subway whenever I needed.

Everything sounded perfect.

But if you've read any of my stories, you already know that "perfect" is never the final word.

The One-Entry Visa I Didn't Know I Had

I went to Hong Kong, dropped off my documents at the Chinese embassy, and planned to return to Shenzhen later that evening. Before heading back, I decided to take a quick shower at the hotel, change clothes, and enjoy one last evening of sightseeing in Hong Kong.

That little decision—to go back for a few more hours—turned out to be a *very* expensive one.

When I returned to the Shenzhen border, tired but content from a day of wandering, the immigration officer took my passport and looked at it longer than usual. I smiled politely, thinking he was just being thorough.

Then he said the words no traveler ever wants to hear: "You cannot enter China."

I blinked, certain he was mistaken. "What do you mean? I just got a new visa at the Chinese embassy."

He shook his head. "Your visa is expired."

My jaw dropped. Apparently, the visa I'd just received was valid for **one entry only**—meant for the sole purpose of re-entering China to finalize my work permit. By leaving again to sightsee, I had unknowingly used up my only allowed entry.

Now, I was officially **stuck in Hong Kong**.

A Parade, a Breakdown, and an Unexpected Kindness

I called my coworker back in China, panicked. She spoke with the officers and even tried to pull some strings through family in the military, but nothing worked. It was the Chinese New Year; every government office was closed.

The Hong Kong immigration officers were sympathetic and helped me contact the American embassy—but it was the *last day before the holidays*. Everything was shutting down for a week.

I had no hotel, no plan, and the clock was ticking.

Desperate, I remembered a girl I had met on the train to Shenzhen. She was visiting her family in Hong Kong. I called her, hoping she might offer advice—or at least a couch for one night.

She agreed to meet me an hour later. I got off at her suggested stop, exhausted and frazzled. Suddenly, a massive parade of dragons and fireworks appeared down the street—it was New Year's Eve. The crowd pressed closer, the noise swelled, and I spotted her across the road.

That's when I burst into tears.

Yes, right there in the middle of a parade, surrounded by dancing dragons, I stood crying like the tragic heroine in a travel comedy.

She ran over, hugged me, and said gently that she couldn't host me at her parents' house—but she'd help me find somewhere to stay. She even lent me cash so I wouldn't get charged foreign transaction fees on my Chinese debit card.

We eventually found a hostel with one last private room left. I spent the night there, grateful beyond words.

Strangers and Small Miracles

The next day, the hostel was fully booked, and I had to move again. While wandering with my luggage, I stopped at a 7-Eleven to think things through. (If you've been to Asia, you know that 7-Eleven isn't just a convenience store—it's practically a lifestyle.)

As I sat outside with a beer, a man approached and asked where I was from. He said he was from Canada and also lived in Beijing. Normally, I'm cautious about strangers, but something about him seemed trustworthy. I told him my situation, and he nodded knowingly.

Apparently, I wasn't the first to fall into this "one-entry visa" trap.

He offered to let me share his hotel room until the embassy reopened. "It's got two beds," he said. "We can split the cost."

It wasn't the most comforting offer from someone I had just met—but hotels were sold out everywhere, and I had no other option. I decided to take the chance.

To my relief, he turned out to be genuinely kind. We became friends, and I ended up spending an unplanned week in Hong Kong, exploring the city while waiting for the embassy to reopen.

Meanwhile, my friend in Beijing managed to retrieve my luggage from the Shenzhen hotel through a relative, who carried it across the border to meet me. I'll never forget that act of kindness—it made me feel less like a stranded foreigner and more like part of a global community of people who care.

When Disaster Turns Into Discovery

Eventually, the Chinese embassy reopened, and I got a new tourist visa—out of my own pocket, of course. When I returned to Beijing, I explained everything to my employer. Luckily, my working visa itself was still valid, so I could complete my work permit after all.

Looking back, that chaotic week in Hong Kong became one of the most memorable experiences of my life. I met strangers who became friends, discovered how resilient I could be under pressure, and learned a lesson that would follow me forever: **always read every detail on a visa—twice.**

What began as a bureaucratic nightmare turned into an unexpected adventure.

Sometimes, getting trapped is just life's way of saying, *"Pause. There's something here for you to see."*

"A good traveler has no fixed plans, and is not intent on arriving."
— Lao Tzu

Chapter 6
When You Have No Idea
What You Just Signed Up For

Life in China had become a blend of unpredictability and wonder. Teaching English wasn't just a job—it was a door that opened me to experiences I never expected. While I taught children in schools during the day, I also gave private lessons to adults in the evenings. And when people found out I was a foreigner teaching English, the offers just poured in. The extra income helped, of course, but even more than that, I got to meet incredible people who soon became much more than students—they became friends.

One of the best tools I discovered while living in China was a site called The Beijinger. You could post your services, find jobs, or connect with locals. It was through this platform that I landed my second job, which turned into a whole new chapter in my Chinese adventure. That's how I met her—my student, a sweet woman with a kind smile and very basic English. At our first meeting, she brought a friend along to help translate. She didn't care much for grammar or academic English; she just wanted to speak and understand others better. For many adult students in China, that's really all they want: to have a conversation without fear.

We began our weekly lessons at her home, just practicing casual conversations. Then, one day, she asked me a question that caught me completely off guard: "Would you like to come on a trip with me?"

Apparently, her team was filming something for tourism promotion in Sichuan, and she thought it would be nice for me to tag along. I had time off for the holiday, and I thought, Why not?

So, the plan was simple—at least on paper. I showed up at her apartment early one morning. She was finishing breakfast with her "sister," who I later realized was just a very close friend. In China, it's common to refer to your best friends as siblings. After breakfast, we packed up and headed to the airport to meet the rest of the film crew. That's when I realized—I didn't know a single person on this trip except her. And barely anyone spoke English. Except for a guy from Hong Kong, and of course, my student, whose English was still developing.

It was awkward at first. The kind of awkward where you smile and nod constantly because you don't understand anything around you. We boarded the plane, and I realized I was probably the only foreigner on it. Five hours later, after a nap and some traditional airplane food I couldn't really identify, we landed. I expected to go straight to a hotel, but instead, a van whisked us off to what looked like a large outdoor garden, where a group of people greeted us with tables full of traditional Chinese dishes. I had no idea what was happening. I just went with it.

That night, I gravitated toward the guy from Hong Kong. He spoke fluent English and had gone to NYU, so we had a hometown connection. He was kind, and more than anything, he made me feel less like an alien dropped in a foreign land. We talked a lot, and from then on, I stuck close to him.

Eventually, we made it to the hotel. I was handed a room key and told to rest—I'd be picked up later for dinner. And just like that, I was swept into this odd little world of filming, language barriers, awkward toasts, and spontaneous friendship.

The next day, my student asked if I'd like to appear in the video her team was working on. I didn't even know what the video was for—something promotional. I just said, sure, why not?

A few days later, I came down to the hotel lobby to find two fancy black cars waiting for us. I got in and felt like I was about to be taken to a red carpet event. When we arrived in a small town, cameras were already rolling and locals were buzzing with excitement. When I stepped out of the car, people swarmed around me, touching my hair like I was some kind of mythical creature. It was surreal. My student and her "sister" took me to a tent shop and asked me to try on a traditional dress from that region. I didn't think I looked particularly good in it, but they loved it and insisted I wear it for the video.

The guy from Hong Kong directed me: "Just act like you're buying something." I stood next to an older man who was supposedly selling goods, but neither of us understood the other. I wasn't sure if he even spoke Mandarin or one of China's many regional dialects. Still, I smiled and played the part.

Later that day, I was told we were having dinner with a very important local official. I didn't know who he was, but I went. His home was warm, inviting, and filled with people. I was seated at the dinner table between the host and my Hong Kong friend. The host offered me baijiu—a

Chinese liquor with a punch that could knock down a horse. I politely declined, knowing how strong it was. So, he brought out a bottle of wine instead. From a wooden box. Just for me. That gesture made me feel deeply welcomed, like I was part of something intimate and special.

The evening became one big blur of cheers, clinking glasses, and countless gānbēi(干杯)—the Chinese word for "cheers," which literally means "dry cup." Every family member came to toast with me, and before I knew it, the entire bottle of wine was gone. I felt fine until I stood up. The room spun. I needed air.

Outside, women in traditional outfits were dancing in a circle near a fire. I didn't hesitate—I ran over and joined them. Even the host and his wife danced with us. It was wild, magical, and joyfully chaotic. The film crew decided to capture it all. We partied until who knows when. Late enough that the memory is just one colorful blur.

The next morning wasn't quite so magical.

I woke up drenched in sweat, my head splitting, barely able to move. Someone was knocking on the door, but I couldn't get up. Eventually, the hotel staff opened the door with a spare key. My student, her "sister," and two hotel employees came in. They helped me change clothes, brought me soup, and gave me medicine. I was completely out of it—embarrassed, exhausted, and deeply hungover.

But even in that state, I felt cared for.

That trip turned into something far bigger than I had expected. I didn't just teach English. I got a glimpse into a world I could never have imagined. I acted in a promotional film. I was treated like a celebrity in a small Chinese town. I danced under firelight with strangers who felt like old friends. And I was reminded again of something important: the most meaningful adventures often begin with a simple Why not?

Chapter 7

Lost in Translation: The Travel Language Gap

I learned quickly that communication abroad isn't just about words. It's about gestures, apps, and the willingness to look a little foolish.

When you first land in a foreign country, you're stripped of your language—and suddenly, even the simplest task becomes a mini mission. Buying water? You mime drinking. Finding a bus? You point, nod, smile. You learn to read faces and trust vibes—sometimes more than translations.

Traveling to a different country can be thrilling—but also frustrating, especially when it comes to communication. It's easy to assume English will carry you everywhere. And yes, it is considered a global language. I always recommend *The Mother Tongue* by Bill Bryson. It's one of my favorite books, and it explains how English became the world's lingua franca, especially in business.

But I don't want to go off track.

The truth is, language can become a real barrier when you're exploring other parts of the world. While English is spoken widely in many communities, that's not always the case. And when you land in one of those beautiful places where no one speaks your language, it can be a challenge. That's why I always suggest being prepared in advance—

especially for moments when you need to communicate something important but don't share a language with the people around you.

I've definitely experienced that discomfort firsthand. Not being able to explain myself clearly—especially when it matters—is unsettling. Over time, I've found a few tools and techniques that help bridge the gap.

Let's start with the obvious: **Google Translate**. While it's not the most efficient or reliable translator out there, it has improved a lot since its early versions. You can definitely use it when you need help, but you have to be smart about it. The key is to use **short, simple sentences**.

Translation apps often struggle with the complexity of language— things like semantics, syntax, and lexical variations. If you type out long or wordy phrases, you're more likely to get an awkward or even completely wrong translation.

Take a simple question like, "Where is the fish market?" Sounds easy enough, right? But once that goes through a translator and starts mixing with foreign verb tenses, articles, or grammar structures, it may not come out right. Instead, try breaking it down. You could rephrase it to "Where fish market?" Or switch the order to "Market fish where?" This stripped-down structure tends to work better because different languages organize their parts of speech differently. The simpler and more direct your sentence, the better chance it has of being understood correctly.

Another useful feature in the Google Translate app is the **camera translation tool**. I really wish I had that back when I was in China, staring blankly at menus I couldn't read. Now, when you download the app, you'll notice a **camera icon** . Just tap it, take a photo of the text, and the app will translate it instantly.

This is great for menus, signs, or product labels. But as with everything else in translation, it isn't always perfect. Sometimes the app can't quite grasp the structure of what it's translating, especially when grammar gets too complex. Still, it gives you enough information to **decipher the message**—and that can make all the difference when you're trying to figure out what dish you just ordered.

If you're willing to spend a bit more, you can look into **translator gadgets**. Google has one called *Pixel Buds* that's received pretty good reviews. I haven't personally tried them yet, but I definitely plan to— and once I do, I'll be sure to share my review. Other brands offer similar tools too, and you can find them on Amazon. Just keep in mind: **they're not flawless**, and like any tool, they can mess up translations. Even with these gadgets, I'd still stick to basic language to improve my chances of being understood.

One habit I recommend—and follow myself—is doing a little **homework before your trip**. It doesn't take much time, and it can make a huge difference. Try to write out a list of the **most essential** travel **phrases**: "Where is the bathroom?", "How much is it?", "What is that?" Think about vocabulary specific to your own needs. For instance, if you're a vegetarian, learn how to say that. If you have allergies, write down how to explain them in the local language.

When I was in China, one thing I noticed was that a lot of food was spicy—everywhere: restaurants, food courts, street vendors. At that time,

I didn't enjoy spicy food at all. (Now, I love it!) So I learned early how to say **"no spicy,"** which in Mandarin is **bù là (不辣)**. Just those two little words saved me from a lot of fiery surprises. And over time, trying new foods and stepping outside my comfort zone even changed my tastes. That's one of the beautiful things about travel—it opens you up, even to flavors you once avoided.

But at the end of the day, the most important thing to remember is this: **you are the visitor.** We can't—and shouldn't—expect people in other countries to learn our language just to accommodate us. They don't have to. That's not their role. We're in *their* country, *their* culture, *their* world.

So be open. Be curious. Even if you're staying somewhere just a few days, try to learn something. It doesn't have to be perfect. You don't have to speak fluently. I'm not saying you need to fully "learn the language," especially if you're only there short term. Learning a new language takes serious discipline, time, and above all, **passion**. But even just a little effort—learning the most common or useful words—will go a long way.

People notice when you try. They appreciate it.

And believe me, it will help you. It will make your trip smoother, more enriching, and full of meaningful interactions that wouldn't happen otherwise.

"You don't need to speak the same language to understand each other— you just need to care enough to try. —**Zhara Michelle York**

Chapter 8
How to Take Your Career Abroad

So, you've made the decision — you want to work overseas. But where do you start? It's a question that stops many people in their tracks. While it might seem like a complicated process, especially if you've never done anything like it before, the truth is: it's more accessible than ever. Thanks to the internet, we now have access to a wide range of global resources that didn't exist years ago.

If you're one of those people who has been daydreaming about moving abroad — about living and working in another country — I want to share what I've learned, what's possible, and how you can start.

Personally, I'm very adventurous. I don't hesitate to pack up and move — whether it's to a new city or an entirely different country. But this mindset comes with one essential requirement: **openness to change**.

Living abroad means adapting. It means sometimes not finding the food you love or the stores you're used to. You might be lucky and discover familiar comforts — but more often, you won't. That's okay. You grow through those differences. And the good news? You'll often find communities of people from your home country, which can help ease the transition. Still, nothing beats approaching this lifestyle with a friendly attitude and a willingness to engage with a different culture. Working overseas is more than just a job; it's an adventure — and you need to be ready for that.

Teaching Abroad

My own journey began as an **English teacher**, working full-time in schools. Once I got settled in each place, I started **networking** —meeting people and taking on **private lessons**. These side gigs were easy to find, especially in countries where English isn't the national language. But here's the thing: you don't have to teach English only. If you speak another language or have a skill, you can teach that too.

There's demand out there — especially for language instruction and exam prep (think IELTS, TOEFL, SAT). Just be aware that **some countries require certification** to teach English, particularly for non native speakers. If you're a native speaker and fluent, a certificate isn't always necessary, but some countries are tightening their policies. Always check the local requirements before diving in.

There are several **certifications** to consider:

- **TEFL** (Teaching English as a Foreign Language)
- **TESL** (Teaching English as a Second Language)
- **TESOL** (Teaching English to Speakers of Other Languages)
- **CELTA** (Certificate in Teaching the English Language to Adults)

Which one you'll need depends on the country and the employer.

That said, you can often teach private lessons **without any certification** — especially if you build a network locally.

I also pursued a **Master's in TESOL**, which can increase your earning potential. But be warned: a U.S.-based Master's program is a serious investment — of both time and money. And the return on that investment isn't always proportional. From personal experience, the salary bump may not justify the cost of the degree.

Some teachers also specialize — for example, in **Business English**, **Legal English**, or **Medical English** — depending on the students' needs. In today's global market, Business English is in especially high demand. If you have niche knowledge, that's a strength you can leverage.

To get started, get to know the **local expat websites**. When I lived in China, *The Beijinger* was incredibly helpful for finding jobs and promoting my services. Don't underestimate how powerful local knowledge and networking can be. Use the internet to connect, promote, and grow.

Going Remote

Working abroad doesn't mean you have to teach — or even have a local job. **Remote jobs** have become more mainstream thanks to tech and globalization.

Fields like IT, graphic design, web development, and **online writing** (blogging, copywriting, technical writing) all offer potential for location-independent careers. Landing one of these jobs can be tough, and I won't sugarcoat it — getting that "perfect remote job" takes work. But it is possible.

Start by building a clear, skill-focused résumé. Apply through international job boards, and if you already have a skill, **promote it**

yourself. Build a profile that targets your ideal clients. I'll include websites I recommend at the end of this chapter — keep reading.

Another remote path is **trading** — in stocks or cryptocurrency. This one isn't easy. In fact, I've tried it, and I'll admit — it's not my strength. But if you're financially savvy, it's worth considering.

There are three types of traders:

- **Position traders:** Long-term investors who wait months or even years.

- **Swing traders:** Those who trade every few days or weeks — usually while holding a full-time job.

- **Day traders:** Full-time, high-risk, fast-paced. This one's for those who thrive on adrenaline and analysis.

If you're looking for a **steady income**, day trading may not be ideal. It's not always reliable. But there's potential for significant earnings — if you're skilled and disciplined. Personally, I still think it's a form of gambling, but some people really do make it work. If you're one of them, it's a job that lets you travel with total freedom.

Nomadic Jobs

Some people thrive with **nomadic work** — taking jobs on the road. These aren't usually career paths but rather temporary roles that offer **cash in hand.**

For example:

- Bartenders

- Musicians

- Caterers

- Lifeguards

- Seasonal farmworkers

- Park attendants

I've met many people who travel the world this way. My stepbrother, for instance, worked as a bartender across Europe. His last stop before settling down was Ibiza.

These jobs often come from **networking in person** — just walking into venues and asking if they need help. Musicians might scout out bars with live music and ask to perform. It's social, informal, and takes a bit of courage. For some people, that's the dream. For me personally, I prefer a bit more stability — but nomadic jobs can also serve as **extra income** while you travel.

Global Positions

Then there are **professional international jobs** — the ones that often come with relocation packages and long-term placements.

Think:

- Diplomats

- International government employees

- Corporate transfers with global companies

I once had a student from Mexico who was relocated to Dubai by his marketing firm. He made business trips across the Middle East and was essentially living globally, all through one employer.

These jobs are not always easy to get. Some require advanced degrees, specific experience, and lots of perseverance. But if you qualify, don't hesitate. These positions often come with major perks — like **paid relocation** — and let you live abroad with security.

If you're serious about landing one, build a strong résumé, tailor it for international roles, and stay persistent.

Helpful Resources

Here are the websites and platforms I've used or recommend to help with your overseas job hunt:

- **Indeed** – International job board with listings in multiple fields

- **Monster** – Similar to Indeed, good for a wide variety of industries.

- **Gold Star Teachers** – Especially useful if you're looking to teach English in China (my first teaching job came from here!)

- **TeachAway** – Lots of global teaching jobs and info on certification requirements.

- **Edvectus** – A recruiter for international schools; selective but legitimate.

- **Fiverr** – Great for freelancers to promote their services and build an online presence.

- **Udemy** – Offers affordable trading courses like Japanese Candlesticks.

- **Piggibacks** – A solid platform for beginners learning to trade.

Important Tip: Never pay a recruiter. Real recruiters are paid by the employer, not you. And no matter which job path you take — **network, network, network**.

Whatever path you choose — teaching, freelancing, corporate, or nomadic — it will require intention and effort. But if you're craving change, if you're ready to experience something new, this might just be your moment. Define your goal. Make a plan. And don't let fear distract you from the path ahead.

A lot of people fail simply because they stop trying. So don't give up. Your job — and your next chapter — might be waiting somewhere far from home.

"Wherever you go, go with all your heart." — **Confucius**

Chapter 9
A Eurotrip Without a Plan

Impromptu — that's the best word to describe it. This trip wasn't planned, scheduled, or debated. It just happened. After the pandemic forced me to pause my overseas adventures in 2020, I was itching to travel again. Like many of us, I had been stuck inside too long. So in 2021, when travel started opening up again, I told myself: it's time.

At first, I just began brainstorming, casually checking flights online with no serious intention. And then — there it was on my screen: Germany. That was it. Decision made. I didn't overthink it. I booked it.

Spontaneity like this is something I've grown to love. These last-minute trips — the ones with no expectations, no rigid plans — always end up being the most exciting and meaningful. I remembered that my stepbrother lived in Germany, so I messaged my stepmother to ask if she wanted me to bring anything to him. He was living in Hamburg, while I was flying into Berlin. They're about three hours apart by road. But I didn't care. This would be the perfect excuse to experience traveling from Berlin to Hamburg by bus.

That's how I like to travel — not with luxury in mind, but by immersing myself in the everyday flow of a place. Sure, I could have booked a train or even a rideshare. In Germany, carpooling is a common way to get around, and it's one of those quirky, local things I love to explore.

As I've shared in other stories, I often book **Airbnb Experiences** when I travel solo. It's a great way to meet people and adds a social dimension to my trips. If you're browsing, look for experiences that include multiple participants. Read the itinerary closely — it'll give you a good idea of what the vibe will be like and whether it's an opportunity to connect with others.

My first tour in Berlin was unforgettable — hands down one of the best I've ever joined. It was called **Rude Bastard Tours of Berlin** — yes, that's really the name. That alone made me curious. This wasn't your typical historical walking tour. It was irreverent, hilarious, and refreshingly unfiltered. At the meeting point, I joined the group and our tour guide, and from the very start, it felt like more than just sightseeing. It was a connection. There was laughter, candid conversation, and zero pressure to be politically correct.

At one point, the guide turned to the group and, with total seriousness, asked, "How do you say 'dick slap' in French?" (Excuse the vulgarity — it was part of the humor.) A French traveler in our group confidently responded: "Biffler." Yes, I learned a new word that day. That little phrase became a running joke among the group — not just for that tour, but through the rest of my Berlin stay. Coincidentally, I ended up crossing paths with that same French guy and another traveler from Southeast Asia on later Airbnb tours. That's the magic of travel: people you randomly meet once can end up becoming part of your trip's story.

The next tour we did together introduced me to something unique to Berlin — the **Späti** kiosks. These little corner shops are where Berliners grab beers and wines on the go, and they've become part of local social culture. They sell drinks for less than 2 euros — perfect if you enjoy sipping as you walk around the city. Even though I'm not really a beer person, I should've made an exception. Germany is synonymous with beer. And while they didn't invent it, they've certainly claimed it as part of their national identity. Beer is to Germany what wine is to France — and yes, there's wine here too, but you won't find it at Spätis.

Our group walked through Berlin, stopping at Spätis, chatting, laughing, and soaking in the city. We ended our route standing somewhere in the street, surrounded by **techno music** — a staple of Berlin's youth culture. This mix of spontaneous walking, drinks, and street parties is how young Berliners hang out. Techno is everywhere here — in bars, in clubs, even outdoors. Berlin isn't just multicultural — it's electric.

After that amazing night, though, I woke up with a killer headache. I hadn't even drunk that much, but I think the wine — and the fact that it probably wasn't great wine — was to blame. I desperately needed painkillers and had to walk ten minutes to find a pharmacy. In that moment, ten minutes felt like a marathon. When I arrived, I asked the pharmacist if she spoke English. Like many Germans I spoke to, she modestly replied, "A little." But then she proceeded to understand everything and speak clearly. In my experience, Germans often underestimate their English — and honestly, many speak it better than people in countries where English is the first language. Just an observation.

She gave me the medicine — even a glass of water — and I slowly started to feel human again. I rested that day, but Berlin wasn't done with me yet.

The next day, I met up with the Southeast Asian traveler again. He and the French guy had stayed in touch and planned to meet two German women we'd all met at the Späti crawl. We were also joined by another guy, originally from Austria, who now lived in Berlin. Our little international group was growing by the day.

We all planned to go to a parade… but we never actually found it. You'd think a parade would be hard to miss. Somehow, we were always walking in the wrong direction. It became a running joke. Eventually, we gave up and headed to **Tiergarten Park**, one of the largest and most beloved green spaces in Berlin. The sun was out, and the weather was perfect.

After a while, the German girls left, and the four of us — me and the three guys — kept exploring. Naturally, food was next. We went to **Curry 36**, one of the most famous spots in Berlin for **currywurst**, a traditional German sausage dish. One of the guys said it was the third most popular spot in the city. I don't know about the rankings, but it was definitely good. We weren't full, though, so we made a pizza stop next.

The Austrian guy eventually said goodbye, and it was just the three of us again. The French traveler suggested one last stop — an outdoor **techno party at Tempelhofer Feld**, a massive park with a rich history (and nearly 1,000 acres of open space). It sounded perfect.

But — like the parade — we couldn't find the party.

Apparently, we arrived too late. One of the locals told us it had already ended. It became clear that while our French friend had a lot of ideas, he wasn't great with directions. Still, his misdirection kept leading us to unexpected fun. So, in a way, I was grateful.

Eventually, we all went our separate ways. I had a **2 a.m. bus to Hamburg**, so I didn't bother going back to my hotel. I found the train, made my way through eerily empty streets, and waited at the station. I boarded my bus and, after a quick glimpse of the German countryside, passed out from exhaustion.

When I arrived in Hamburg, I messaged my stepbrother. It was our first time meeting in person. I took the subway to his neighborhood, met him and his family, and spent a lovely day before heading back to Berlin. My flight to New York was early the next morning.

And that was the trip — a totally unplanned, whirlwind journey that ended up being one of the most refreshing, spontaneous experiences I've ever had. This is how I travel: with no overthinking, no fuss, and no checklist. I go where my gut takes me. And every time, I come back with more stories than I ever expected.

Useful Sources

- **Rude Bastards Tour of Berlin** – Also available on Airbnb. Highly recommended for open-minded travelers.

- **Curry 36** – For authentic currywurst and German sausage.

- **Späti Crawl** – Try an Airbnb Späti kiosk crawl to experience Berlin's casual night scene.

- **Hip Berlin Underground Tour** – A graffiti and street culture walking tour.

- **Tempelhofer Feld** – A vast public park rich with history, popular for outdoor techno events.

Disclaimer: Some names and identifying details have been changed to protect the privacy of individuals. Any resemblance to real persons, living or dead, is purely coincidental.

"It feels good to be lost in the right direction." — **Unknown**

Chapter 10
No Plan, Just Dubai

My experience living in Dubai was a wild odyssey — but then again, most of my life seems to unfold that way. When I moved there, I didn't have a clear plan. I left with about $10,000 in savings, two suitcases of belongings, and zero guarantees. No job, no housing. It was a decision driven more by emotion than logic. I was going through a difficult time emotionally and knew I needed to be somewhere — anywhere — other than home.

In hindsight, sure, things might have gone differently with a stable plan. But that wasn't my story. What I did have was determination and a willingness to leap.

Getting Settled

Like any country, moving to the UAE means navigating paperwork. The process of getting legal documentation — residency, work permits, IDs — depends on whether you're self-employed or working for a company. Either way, the process isn't as tough as it can be elsewhere as long as you're willing to pay.

In Dubai, nearly everything revolves around **money**, especially for foreigners. It's a trade-off: there's no income tax, but you'll pay fees for almost every government-related service you can imagine.

My decision to move came after a vacation I'd taken in Dubai earlier that year. I'd made a few friends during that trip and reached out to them before I arrived. One of them, a girl I'd met on an overnight desert tour, came to pick me up from the airport. Another, a guy I'd connected with through someone else on that trip, also met me there — it was our first time meeting in person.

They were both helpful at first. The girl let me rent a room in her apartment at a very affordable rate. The guy drove me there and offered to help me find a job — though nothing ever came of that. In the end, I found work on my own.

Employment & Housing in the UAE

I stayed in that apartment and immediately started my job search. A couple of weeks before my move, I'd begun applying online. I asked the friend I was staying with if I could use her phone number and Dubai address on my résumé to make it look more local — and more attractive to employers. Some companies prefer candidates already in-country since they don't have to cover flights or relocation.

In the UAE, many expats arrive on a tourist visa and job hunt once they're there. You're allowed to stay for a certain number of days, and if you don't secure a job, you either leave and re-enter or apply for a visa extension (which, of course, comes with a fee). Overstaying results in daily fines — again, more money.

The truth is, **if you can pay**, you're rarely punished with deportation. You can enter, leave, return, and reset the clock — as long as you're covering the costs. Still, factors like nationality and passport strength can influence this process, so always check the UAE's official visa information before making a move.

In hindsight, waiting for a company to offer me a job from abroad — ideally one that covered flights and relocation — would have been the smarter option. But I couldn't wait. I needed out. I was impatient and determined.

When I arrived, I printed stacks of résumés and spent entire days walking around Dubai, handing them out — hotels, schools, real estate offices, tour companies, you name it. But my strongest background was in education, so I eventually focused on schools again. Time was ticking, and so was my visa.

Meanwhile, the apartment I was staying in was not ideal. Though I was grateful for the low rent, the neighborhood was in **Sharjah**, another Emirate with a more traditional and conservative vibe. It felt far from the version of Dubai I had experienced on vacation. The architecture, pace, and even culture were completely different — and I didn't feel at home.

I needed to move. But with no job and no income, it probably looked irrational to go apartment hunting. I did it anyway. I refused to give up. One morning, I told myself I'd find a place that day —and I did. I found a small apartment in an area I liked, with affordable rent. The landlord was kind and agreed to let me pay in cash until my residence documents were sorted.

Then, while out distributing résumés, I got a text from my friend — a **school** had called the number I'd listed on my applications. They wanted to schedule an interview. I called back immediately.

There was just one issue: the school was located in **Ajman**, another Emirate, nearly an hour from my new apartment. But I didn't care. I needed the job. I interviewed the next day and got the position almost immediately. They needed staff urgently.

I had housing, and I had work. Next, I needed a car.

A guy I'd met through the friend I initially stayed with ran a small car rental business with his brother. I'd borrowed a car from him before, so I asked if it was for sale. It was — and we worked out a deal. Within 30 days of arriving, I had an apartment, a job, and a car.

The Emirates ID — Your Life on a Card

To live in the UAE, you need an **Emirates ID**. It's your identity, your key to everything — housing, banking, healthcare, even driving.

Without it, you're invisible.

Once I started working, getting my Emirates ID became my top priority. I needed it to open a bank account, issue monthly rent checks (which are still required there), and register the car in my name. Until then, I paid the landlord in cash and drove the car under the seller's registration — both thanks to people who trusted me. That isn't always the case, so I was fortunate.

But my school took forever to process the paperwork. It was frustrating. I wasn't the only one — other teachers were also waiting. Apparently, it had something to do with licensing issues between Ajman and Dubai. Each Emirate has different rules.

I later learned that my school had applied for a **work visa under a different job title** because the teaching license process was so delayed. It was disappointing. In the UAE, your visa includes your job title. And your visa ties you legally to your employer — you can't legally work elsewhere.

What's worse: **leaving a job isn't easy**. If you're under a **limited contract,** breaking it can lead to huge penalties. These contracts often match your visa's duration — two or three years, depending on the employer's location. (Mainland companies offer 2-year visas; free zones often issue 3-year visas.)

Thankfully, my contract was **unlimited,** with a 30-day notice clause. That gave me some flexibility. Once I saw the red flags with that employer, I started looking for a new job. I found one — at a better school, in Dubai, with a higher salary and a shorter commute.

Everything looked promising. I even met a few Americans working there, which was refreshing since expats from the U.S. are rarer in the UAE, especially in Ajman.

Visa Games & Labor Woes

When I resigned from my first job, I learned just how manipulative employers can be.

They **took my passport**, refusing to return it unless I showed a plane ticket or a new job contract. That's illegal — but they did it anyway. They also tried to withhold part of my final paycheck. I was supposed to be paid through the end of my contract, including the holiday period.

When I returned from a trip, I opened a case with the UAE's labor department — but that led nowhere. The law can be vague and slow. And the truth is, in many cases, **power and money win**. This was a monarchy, after all. I was just a guest.

Eventually, I got my passport back, and my pay — but not without a fight. Sadly, my experience wasn't unique.

At my second job, history repeated itself. They delayed issuing my visa. I had to push and pressure them again. Employers can't legally have you work without a visa — but they often do.

Then, a few months later, just after returning from a holiday trip, I was **let go**. No reason. No warning. I wasn't the only one — the school had downsized. In the UAE, most contracts include a **three-month probation period**. During that time, either party can end the agreement without cause or penalty.

Just like that, I was unemployed. And, again, I needed a new job — and a new visa.

I canceled a planned trip to Spain. I was too stressed. A friend invited me to Thailand, but I couldn't enjoy it. I had to return to Dubai and start over.

Eventually, I found work at a **language school in a free zone**. I hoped it would be more professional. It wasn't.

The schedule was chaotic — part-time, on-call, and disorganized. I'd teach for two hours in the morning, then have a four-hour gap, then return at night. I had to pay for parking out of pocket. No reimbursement. No stability. Eventually, I had to leave — and this time, I did so quietly.

If you **leave the UAE for over six months**, your visa is automatically canceled. I emailed my employer to inform them I wasn't returning. They weren't pleased because they couldn't cancel the visa without me in person. But after six months, it would be void anyway. I was done.

The Bigger Picture

In the UAE, quitting a job **without notice** while still in the country can result in your employer filing an **absconding case** — yes, that's a real thing. It wasn't my situation, but it shows how **intense and employer controlled** the system can be.

You can also get residency through a **spouse**, but you'll need a "No Objection Certificate" from them to work. I saw this play out for some married women. Whether it works the other way around — husbands needing permission from wives — I'm not so sure.

Driving in the UAE

To drive legally, you need an Emirates ID — unless you're from certain countries like the U.S., U.K., or Australia. In that case, you can **transfer** your license by taking an eye exam, submitting an application, and paying a fee. Others need to start from scratch — and often need a **no objection letter from their employer** just to apply.

Driving also comes with rules: **every speeding violation is recorded by cameras**, not cops. Your license plate is photographed, and you receive the fine **via text message**. If you lend your car to someone and they speed? The fine still goes to you.

But here's a trick: wait to pay your fines. If you hold off for a bit, the government might issue a discount. I learned this by accident one month when I delayed paying. When I checked again, the fine was cheaper. Small wins!

Living in Dubai taught me a lot. It opened my eyes to a very different way of life — one that's thrilling, challenging, and sometimes maddening. But I also met good people who helped me, offered kindness, and made my time there unforgettable.

Would I do it again? I don't know. But I'd never erase it. *"Oh, the places you'll go."* — Dr. Seuss

Disclaimer: *Some names and identifying details have been changed to protect the privacy of individuals. Any resemblance to real persons, living or dead, is purely coincidental.*

Chapter 11

Chasing Northern Lights and Facing the Unknown

Everything started years ago when I was a child. I remember reading about the Aurora. This natural phenomenon is a magical event that occurs in the northern and southern latitudes of our beautiful planet Earth. I had waited so long to see it, and I decided it was time to chase the Northern Lights, since I lived closer to them than the Southern ones. I chose Alaska. But before undergoing this beautiful experience, there were some ventures along the journey—as always.

A Quick Stop in Seattle

I found a flight with a nine-hour layover in Seattle, which I took as an opportunity to sightsee. I visited the famous Space Needle. Honestly, it felt like just another tall tower—I had seen taller ones before. But the view was beautiful. If you plan to visit, it's better to buy tickets at the gate instead of online, since the website may not reflect accurate schedules.

After that visit, I returned to the airport to catch my flight to Fairbanks, Alaska. Taking a second flight at night after walking around Seattle all day was exhausting. The time difference was only three hours, but the long transfer and all the walking made it feel much longer. Despite the fatigue, I was excited to arrive and explore over the next three days.

Arriving in Fairbanks

Once I landed, I went to the car rental counter. It was late at night, and the airport was surprisingly busy. When it was my turn, the agent told me my reservation had mistakenly been booked for the following month. Thankfully, she found a car for me. But then came the real challenge: driving to the cabin.

The snow was relentless—it looked like a storm. Roads were covered, and it was pitch dark. I followed the GPS, unsure of where I was. Finally, I reached what seemed like the cabin area, but none of the cabins matched my reservation. I saw only what the headlights revealed: snow, pine trees, and a few cabins with lights on. I stepped out of the car to look around. Everything was quiet. There were cars parked, but I didn't hear or see anyone. I wondered if anyone was even inside. For a few moments, fear took over. I was in the middle of nowhere, alone, and my mind went wild with thoughts of serial killers. It may sound funny now, but at the time, it was terrifying.

I messaged the host through the Airbnb app, even though it was 2:30 a.m. Unsurprisingly, there was no reply. Eventually, after circling again, I found the cabin. Relief washed over me—until I realized I had no food or drinks. I had forgotten to stop for snacks or water. I went back out, but everything was closed. Not even gas stations were open. Thankfully, the hosts had left drinking water in the cabin.

Life in a Dry Cabin

This was my first time staying in a dry cabin—common in Alaska but a surprise to me. I hadn't fully read the listing and only noticed the details days before arriving. I messaged the host, who probably thought I was silly for not reading the ad properly. But I did some research and learned dry cabins are typical in Alaska. Some don't even have electricity and rely on generators. Luckily, my cabin had power.

But no running water meant no indoor toilet or shower. There was a toilet—but outside. To use it, I had to bundle up in snow gear and boots and walk outside in the freezing cold. Definitely not ideal for nighttime bathroom trips. I recommend not drinking too many liquids before bed!

For showers, the host recommended nearby recreation centers. Mary Siah Recreation Center charged $4 for showers, or $2 for seniors. The University of Alaska Fairbanks' Student Recreation Center cost $10 a day but included full facility access. I also used Planet Fitness since I had a membership. The downside was having to drive each time, so it was best to get everything done during one visit.

Skiing in Fairbanks

I had booked a ski experience through Airbnb, scheduled for 11:30 a.m. The location seemed close, but I left early due to the snowy roads. The GPS kept directing me to paths blocked by snow. I called the host—let's call her *Heather*—for help.

Heather was incredibly helpful and gave me the address of a nearby restaurant to wait in. Ironically, it was closed—but the cannabis store across the street was open. I guess it counts as an essential business. I tried a café 10 minutes away, but the road conditions delayed me further.

While driving back, I nearly crashed into another car. Shaken, I took a breath. That's when Heather texted that she was nearby. I explained the delay and hurried back. Meeting her was a huge relief—finally, someone local!

Following her made the drive easier. She navigated the storm like it was nothing. Once we arrived at the ski area, I felt calm again. It was my first time skiing, and Heather made it easy and fun—even therapeutic. When we returned, she mentioned she had lost her phone somewhere in the snow but would go back to find it. I couldn't believe how calm she was. I would've panicked!

The Aurora Borealis Experience

To see the Northern Lights, I booked a tour with *Eric* from a company called Face the Outdoors. We met at 8:00 p.m. and would return around 5:00 a.m. If your stay is within Fairbanks city limits, Eric will pick you up. I was outside the area, so I drove to the first pickup point. It was only a 15-minute drive.

The drive to his house took about two hours. It was worth it. His place had huge glass windows perfect for viewing the sky. He served snacks and hot drinks and helped us with camera settings.

Seeing the lights was surreal. You can't see the full colors with your eyes. They appear as a white or light band, but the camera captures vivid greens, pinks, and purples. Why? Because our eyes don't detect color well at night.

With long exposure, the camera reveals what we can't see.

The lights appear in bursts—sometimes five to twenty minutes at a time. You need patience and a little luck. Eric's home was remote, surrounded by wildlife. Though it felt wild, it was safe—animals tend to stay hidden in the cold.

I left that night in awe. Nature had delivered.

A Scheduling Blunder

The next day, I was exhausted. We got back at 4:00 a.m., and I had a flight at noon. Or so I thought.

I arrived early, returned my car, and went through security. At the gate, I was told I had missed my flight. Turns out, it was scheduled for *midnight*, not *noon*. The airline had sent me a check-in message the night before, which should've clued me in.

I was upset, but the airline agent helped me get on the 3:00 p.m. flight— with better seats! Still, I had to wait at the airport for four hours. The time difference between Alaska and New York meant I'd arrive a full day later than expected.

The Spirit of Alaska

Even though I wasn't there long, I felt the warmth of Alaskans. People waved as I drove past. I saw a stranger pull over to help a cab driver stuck in the snow. Small gestures, but meaningful.

One of my favorite spots was a Mediterranean restaurant called Spice It Up . The food—especially the gyros and garlic naan—was incredible. Staff were kind and welcoming. I visited more than once, and each time, I saw a steady stream of customers.

Alaska gave me memories I'll never forget. And if you ever visit, bring warm boots, a good camera, and an open heart. This is a place where nature humbles you, people surprise you, and the skies light up in ways you didn't know were possible.

"The most beautiful thing in the world is, of course, the world itself."—
Wallace Stevens

Disclaimer: *Some names and identifying details have been changed to protect the privacy of individuals. The events described are based on true experiences and intended for storytelling purposes only.*

Chapter 12
Lost and Found in Venice

Impromptu trips are my favorite. After graduating from college—four long years of full-time school and work—I wanted to give myself a well deserved gift: travel. Italy immediately came to mind, especially because my father had a friend living in Milan. That made the first stop easy to decide.

Europe has always fascinated me. Its history, especially in Italy, is everywhere you look. The home of the Roman Empire, rich in art, science, and philosophy—you name it. But I won't make this a history lesson. I just want you to understand how much you can see and learn when you step into the old continent.

When I landed in Milan, it was my first time ever in Europe. I was excited beyond words. My father's friend— let's call him *Marco*— couldn't pick me up, but he gave me clear directions. I hopped on a bus from the airport, naively speaking English to everyone like it was the official language. Reality hit quickly, and I had to put my Italian to use.

Marco hosted me for the first night and took me to a trattoria—a casual Italian restaurant serving local food. The server didn't ask what we wanted to drink, but rather what kind of wine: "Rosso o bianco?" No water, just wine. I quickly learned that in Italy, a good glass of wine is essential to a good meal. And the pasta I had that day? Possibly the best I've ever tasted.

After lunch, we went sightseeing and, of course, stopped for coffee. Italians drink it strong—tiny cups, bold flavors. As someone used to American-style coffee (light and large), it was a culture shock. I asked for an Americano with a little milk and three sweeteners, which earned me a baffled look from the barista. Eventually, I gave in to the Italian way.

Since Marco could only host me that one night, I needed other accommodations. I stayed in three different places in Milan. The first hotel was cozy but a bit pricey, so I downgraded. My next stop was a hostel—my first and last time staying in one alone, or at least that's what I thought. Sharing a room and bathroom with six strangers is not my idea of fun. Bunk beds, an outside bathroom, and zero privacy? No thanks. I stayed there one night. Still, I learned that sometimes you have to do what you have to do. As you'll see from my stories, I've adapted as each experience comes.

The final hostel was slightly better. I got a private bathroom, though it was still outside the room. I had to carry my clothes with me to avoid parading through strangers in a towel. I booked it through Star Hostel Milano—a decent spot if you're on a budget.

Since Marco lived with roommates and couldn't host me again, I decided to explore more. I picked Venice as my next destination and planned a day trip. I bought a train ticket early in the morning, aiming to make the most of the day. The ride was two and a half hours.

The moment I stepped off the train in Venice, I felt disoriented from a nap I had taken. I nearly ended up on the wrong train because I woke up groggy and confused. Once I got my bearings, I searched for an exit. I instinctively looked for the Spanish word "salida," but in Italy, it's "uscita." This mix-up had me wandering around the station like a lost puppy.

Once outside, Venice greeted me with its undeniable beauty. But I was alone. Solo travel has its moments of awkwardness—no one to share the excitement with, just you and your thoughts. I walked a lot. I don't recall how much exactly, but it was nonstop until late evening.

At the end of the day, I sat at a local café with a glass of wine, soaking in the atmosphere. It was peaceful until I realized my train back to Milan was about to depart. Panic set in. My phone was dying. I rushed to find the station but struggled to get directions. Ironically, in a tourist-heavy city like Venice, I couldn't find anyone who spoke English or knew their way around.

I resorted to my broken Italian and asked a man sweeping a sidewalk for help. He gave me directions that, thankfully, I understood. But I arrived just in time to watch my train leave the station.

No economy tickets were left for the rest of the day. My only option? A pricey first-class ticket. I wasn't thrilled, but it was still cheaper than booking a hotel in Venice. I took the first-class ride back to Milan.

And then I got lost—again. Even after charging my phone and calling Marco for help, I couldn't find the bus stop he directed me to. In Milan, street names are posted on building walls, not street poles like in New York. At night, with poor lighting and faint lettering, it was almost impossible to spot them.

While on the phone with Marco, I finally boarded the right bus. A man sitting nearby struck up a conversation—in Italian, of course. It turned into my longest Italian conversation ever. He even offered to help me find my stop. I was skeptical, but Marco called again and asked to speak to him. After confirming the stranger's intentions, I let him guide me.

Eventually, I reached the stop, and Marco was waiting there.

That day in Venice, I met locals, struggled with the language, got lost, and found my way back. It was raw, real, and unforgettable. The best surprises often come when you least expect them—when you're off script and open to whatever the road brings.

Chapter 13
The London Shift

Buckle up, because this trip wasn't just another stamp in my passport—it was a wake-up call I didn't know I needed. I had just moved from the city that never sleeps—New York—to Nashville, Tennessee. Saying goodbye to the apartment I loved, watching my New York ID get replaced, and embracing the quieter life down South was jarring—but necessary. It felt like the right move to realign my financial goals and build something more sustainable.

Still, after all the unpacking, adjusting, and mental recalibrating, I was burnt out. I craved that buzz only a new place could offer. That's when the idea of London popped into my head. Flights were cheaper from New York than from Nashville, so I figured—why not swing by the city that raised me before heading across the pond?

After landing in NYC, I checked into the historic White Horse Tavern and met some old friends. That night was full of laughter and nostalgia. No matter how far I roam, New York always reminds me who I am at my core. I stayed at a friend's place the night before flying out from Newark—and then, it was London time.

Delayed but Determined

I was supposed to land in London at 7:40 PM, but thanks to a plane malfunction, I didn't arrive until 11:30 PM. Hungry, jet-lagged, and annoyed, I realized just how much I missed New York's 24/7 food and transportation. London was asleep—and I was wide awake with a rumbling stomach.

Still, I had a plan: shake off the jet lag with a morning run in Green Park. I'd signed up for a guided running tour through Airbnb and was set to meet a local guide named Mike. The next morning, despite barely sleeping, I laced up and met him by the Buckingham Palace exit of Green Park Station.

Mike was one of those rare people who could hold a full conversation while running. Me? I was huffing and puffing just to keep up. But he made it fun. He even walked me to my next meeting point after the run and gave me tips on exploring the city. We exchanged info and agreed to meet again if he ever visited Nashville.

The Marathon of Sightseeing

Right after the run, I jumped into a second tour. My scheduling skills were clearly ambitious. This one was a more traditional sightseeing tour—walking, learning, and soaking in the history. I wasn't thrilled to feel like a typical tourist, but the guide, Calvin, made it enjoyable with his charisma and storytelling. We didn't exchange contacts, but it was a good vibe overall.

That night, I could barely move. My legs were shot, my shoulders sore, and my eyes heavy. I passed out as soon as I hit the hotel bed.

A French Invitation

The next day brought another tour—and this time, I clicked with a lovely couple from southern France. They were retired, friendly, and living the kind of travel-filled life I dreamed of. We swapped numbers, and they invited me to visit their home near Toulouse and Marseille, promising good wine and great company. It's hard to say no to invitations like that, especially when your heart is already wandering.

Later that evening, I had one more walking tour booked. I was completely drained, but I pushed myself to go. I grabbed dinner at a Turkish spot and met the group. I could barely keep my eyes open. By the end of those two hours, I wasn't even pretending to enjoy myself anymore—I was just waiting for the signal that it was over.

Bar Crawl, British Style

After taking a rest day to journal and reflect, I geared up for something different: a London bar crawl. If you've ever read my Germany stories, you know I'm no stranger to these events—but the British version had its own flair.

Bar crawls are more than drinking. They're social rituals where strangers become friends over shots and shared laughter. The crowd that night was friendly, relaxed, and diverse in age and background. By the end, we were dancing and swapping stories like old pals. I even connected with a local who followed up with me two days later.

Chaos and Kindness

We decided to meet again, but London had other plans—a train strike. That meant I had to take a bus, but I boarded the wrong one. After a series of delays, crowded stops, and one very creepy alley walk, I found a functioning train line and finally made it to our meeting spot.

That night's bar crawl wasn't as magical. The crowd was younger, the energy off. My new local friend and his American buddy were the only people I really talked to. But there was one funny moment: a very drunk woman kept repeating the host's announcements and caused a mini scene at one of the bars. We couldn't help but laugh.

A Sweet Goodbye

It was late. My friend walked me to the bus and even rode a few stops with me to make sure I was okay. He greeted some bar staff like old friends along the way—he was clearly a regular. One of the women he knew helped me get back to my hotel once I transferred buses. That night, I finally slept soundly.

The next day, I saw familiar faces from the bar crawl at another event. One host remembered my name. It made me feel like a local. I met my friend again that evening and had one last dinner with the group. But emotionally, I was in a different place.

The Shift

Something changed during that trip. As I packed for home, I couldn't ignore how different I felt —not just physically drained, but mentally and emotionally pulled in a new direction. I started questioning the career path I was on. I wasn't sure how I would do it, but I knew I had to change something.

That's the thing about travel : when you step outside your routine, you start seeing life from a broader perspective. Your mind stretches. You reflect. You expand. And in those quiet moments between flights and foreign streets, you realize just how big your life can become.

Chapter 14
Submerged in Harmony

After London, something shifted in me. That trip stirred up more than jet lag—it awakened questions I had buried for too long. As I boarded my flight back to the States, I couldn't help but reflect on how travel had become more than a break from routine. It had become a mirror. Each new destination reflected something about myself I hadn't seen clearly before.

The more I traveled, the more I tried new things—almost without thinking. Somewhere along the line, I stopped just exploring places and started exploring parts of *me* I didn't even know existed. And that's what led me, surprisingly, to the ocean.

I used to avoid the water. I wasn't the type to get excited about sea creatures or ocean waves. A beach day for me meant soaking up the sun, sipping a drink, and lounging with a good book—not swimming with fish. But all that changed in Cozumel.

How It All Began

Cozumel has always been a tropical escape for me. The weather, the beaches, the vibrant nature—it had a way of pulling me back again and again. But on this particular visit, something was different. I found myself wanting more than relaxation. I wanted to **dive into the unknown**—quite literally.

It started after chatting with some local friends. They spoke about the underwater world with such wonder and reverence that I couldn't help but be curious. One thing led to another, and soon I was connected to a scuba instructor through a friend of mine.

I wasn't certified yet, but I didn't care. I needed to experience what they were describing. I agreed to meet the instructor at a quiet beach spot and try my very first dive—from the shore. It felt less intimidating that way.

As I stood on the sand, listening to the basics of scuba diving, I could feel anticipation building. The rhythm of the ocean was hypnotic. Every sound—the waves, the wind—seemed to sync with my heartbeat. Even before stepping into the water, I felt a strange connection forming.

The First Descent

The moment I submerged, the world changed.

Everything—noise, pressure, even time—seemed to disappear. I floated in a peaceful, weightless silence that made everything above the surface feel irrelevant. Colorful marine life danced all around me in fluid harmony. I wasn't just visiting—I was part of the ocean now, and the ocean was welcoming me.

That first dive turned my world upside down. I had gone from someone indifferent to ocean life to someone in love with it.

Becoming Certified

I only had a week left in Cozumel, but that didn't stop me. I was determined to get certified so I could dive anywhere on my own. One morning over breakfast, I called PADI, and they explained everything. It turned out the whole process only took three days—and I could complete it all through a local dive school.

That's how I met **Ernesto**, my instructor at Island Divers Cozumel. He wasn't just a skilled diver—he was calm, patient, and genuinely passionate about the ocean. No ego. No showmanship. Just pure love for diving and a desire to share it. Under his guidance, I completed my training : two dives a day, practice exercises, and a written test that wasn't even about passing or failing. If you got something wrong, he simply explained it until you understood. It was that simple.

Night Diving: Another World Below

Even after I completed my certification, I wasn't done. I signed up for a night dive—and that, too, blew my mind.

Night diving is a completely different experience. As twilight faded, the ocean transformed. Nocturnal creatures emerged, glowing and gliding like characters in a deep-sea fairytale. With visibility reduced, we relied on flashlights strapped to our wrists and hand signals to communicate. It was eerie—but beautiful.

Yes, part of me was nervous. The dark ocean brings all kinds of "what ifs" to mind. But the buddy system is everything. With someone by your side, it becomes less about fear and more about **shared awe**. Every sound, every shimmer of bioluminescent light, felt like stepping into a secret world few ever get to see.

The Power of the Team

One of the biggest surprises of diving is how connected it makes you feel—not just to the ocean, but to people.

Diving is not a solo sport —not if you're doing it right. Each time you dive, you're paired with others—sometimes strangers, but by the time you resurface, it feels like you've known them forever. You bond through trust, teamwork, and a kind of silent communication that doesn't exist on land.

It doesn't matter who you are or where you come from. In the water, we're all the same—explorers sharing space with nature, each other, and something much bigger than ourselves.

Lessons from the Ocean

The ocean taught me things I didn't know I needed to learn.

I saw how fish swim in schools without ever colliding, how species give each other space without judgment, and how the rules of nature are based on **respect**. They don't touch unless necessary. They don't intrude. They move together—but freely. It's as if a quiet understanding exists between them.

There's a peace to it—a reminder that harmony is possible. The sea showed me that boundaries matter. That coexistence is beautiful. That we don't need to control everything to belong.

A Sanctuary for the Soul

In the ocean, I found a sanctuary. A place where I didn't have to explain myself, where nobody expected anything from me. No roles to play. No one in my space. Just me, the water, and the quiet rhythm of life moving all around me.

It became more than a sport or a thrill. It was healing. Transformational. It made me feel connected to something deeper—something ancient and true.

"When anxious, uneasy and bad thoughts come, I go to the sea, and the sea drowns them out with its great wide sounds, cleanses me with its noise, and imposes a rhythm upon everything in me that is bewildered and confused." — Rainer Maria Rilke

Travel brought me to this. Not just physically, but emotionally. If I hadn't wandered, I wouldn't have discovered diving. If I hadn't been curious, I'd still be lounging on beaches with no idea what magic lay beneath them. Every country, every culture, every person I've met has opened a door to a new version of myself.

London reminded me to chase freedom.

Cozumel reminded me to **immerse myself in it.**

That's the gift of travel. It expands your mind. It stretches your soul. It shows you who you are—if you let it.

Chapter 15
The Courage to Wander Alone

There's something about being underwater—alone with your breath and the rhythm of the sea—that mirrors the experience of traveling alone. That sense of peace and trust in your own rhythm stayed with me, even when I was thousands of miles away from the ocean. In that same spirit of independence, I began embracing the world on my own terms.

Solo travel isn't a backup plan for when no one else can come along. It's an intentional choice—a bold act of self-love, confidence, and curiosity. Over the years, my solo journeys have become more than just travel experiences. They've become personal growth accelerators, helping me face uncertainty, embrace cultural differences, and learn to truly enjoy my own company.

There's something about the quiet moments of travel that reveal more than any postcard-perfect view ever could. After so many shared experiences, social adventures, and chance connections across continents, I've come to deeply value another kind of journey—one where it's just me, my thoughts, and the wide-open world. The truth is, some of the most exhilarating experiences don't require a companion. In fact, traveling alone has often gifted me the most profound discoveries, both outward and inward.

I know the feeling all too well—the challenge of finding someone whose enthusiasm matches yours, whose schedule aligns, or who simply has the courage to leap into the unknown. But I promise, you don't need to wait. The world is yours, and solo travel opens up a kind of freedom that's impossible to replicate when your plans are tied to someone else.

Picture it: every decision is yours, every detour is welcome, and every encounter, no matter how brief, belongs entirely to your own narrative.

I've had the privilege of following my wanderlust wherever it called—from spontaneous escapes across European landscapes to carefully planned itineraries through nature's most breathtaking wonders. Going solo has consistently turned out to be one of the most thrilling decisions I've ever made. You don't just visit new places—you meet new versions of yourself.

Like Buddha once said, "Travel only with thy equals or thy betters; if there are none, travel alone." There's empowerment in that truth.

One of my favorite memories was in Beijing, China. I had become obsessed with bubble milk tea—absolutely smitten. But those Mandarin tones? A real struggle. I didn't want to butcher the name every time I ordered, so I came up with a quirky little trick. I'd silently hum the name to myself—Zhen Zhu Nai Cha (珍珠奶茶)—matching each syllable to its tone like a song. It became my secret melody of confidence, a private rehearsal before stepping up to the counter with pride. It's a small example, but it captures what solo travel is all about: finding your own way to make unfamiliar places feel a bit more like home.

And language isn't the only thing that can trip you up abroad. Cultural differences are their own glorious, often comical surprises. Like the time I first lived in China and greeted people with a friendly kiss-blow on the cheek. Oops. Apparently not the standard hello. Lesson learned—quickly. I adapted to the more reserved greeting style and saved myself from future awkward encounters.

Then there was Dubai. Every time I stopped at a gas station—even at self-service ones—a man would rush over to fill up my car. At first, I was confused. I didn't see other men getting the same treatment. Soon I realized: that's just how it works there. In many aspects of life, men take care of women. Sometimes it was helpful, sometimes a little annoying, but I respected the cultural norm and rolled with it.

That's why I always say—do your research before you go. Not just about what to pack or what to see, but about how people live. It helps avoid those "oops" moments and makes interactions more meaningful. You're not just a visitor—you're a guest.

When it comes to planning solo trips, I like to leave room for both structure and surprise. Yes, I do my homework. I check out the must sees, figure out transportation, and map my goals. But I also give myself permission to wander. The joy of solo travel is the space it creates to go off script—to wake up one day and follow a whim.

One app I've loved for meeting people abroad is Meetup. It's free and full of events tailored to whatever you're into. I once joined a language exchange meetup and ended up connecting with amazing people from around the world. I've gone to happy hours, art tours, outdoor runs—there's always something going on, and you're never really alone if you don't want to be.

Airbnb has also been a surprising gem—not just for places to stay, but for experiences. I usually book a few activities at the start of a trip. It helps me get oriented and meet people with similar interests. Once in Germany, I booked three tours and ended up seeing the same two travelers on the second one. By the third, we were fast friends. That night we all joined a wild bar crawl. The next day, we explored again and added even more new friends to the mix. None of it was planned—but those spontaneous connections are what I cherish most.

And while solo travel is incredibly liberating, it's also great for budgeting. No splitting bills, no compromising on where to eat or what to do—you're in full control. That includes being smart with money.

I'll admit, I'm not a die-hard hostel girl. Sharing a bathroom and room with strangers? Not my idea of relaxing. But some hostels let you book private rooms for a bit more, while still giving you the community vibe. It's worth asking questions before you book to make sure it's the right fit.

One of my favorite ways to explore a culture is through its food. I love local eateries—street food stands, hole-in-the-wall spots, those places only locals know. Sure, sometimes it's intimidating to order in another language, but having a shortlist of phrases really helps. And who knows? You might find your new favorite dish.

Transportation is another place to save. Walk when you can. Take public transit. Not only do you save money, but you also get a feel for the everyday rhythm of the place you're visiting. Some of my best discoveries happened just from wandering aimlessly through streets I'd never seen before.

When booking flights, I've learned a few clever tricks. Booking in advance helps, of course. But using a VPN to change your virtual location to the destination country can sometimes show cheaper prices from local airlines. It's not a magic fix, but it's a handy hack to try.

And yes, set a daily budget. Track your spending. I know it doesn't sound fun, but it gives you freedom—freedom to splurge when it matters and peace of mind that you're not going broke while sipping wine in a piazza.

But let's talk safety too. Solo travelers need to stay alert. Trust your gut. Don't take sketchy offers. Protect your valuables. Read about common scams in the area. The more informed you are, the more confident— and safer—you'll feel.

Beyond all the logistics and life hacks, solo travel is a journey inward. It's about reconnecting with your own rhythm. I've had moments of deep reflection, sipping tea in a foreign café, or sitting in silence under unfamiliar stars. These moments are likesoul whispers. They nudge you toward clarity. They remind you of who you are and who you want to be.

And the people you meet—wow. There's a magic in the connections you make on the road. Some people have become lifelong friends. We still keep in touch, even years later. We've visited each other's homes, shared milestones, and stayed in each other's lives. Travel doesn't just expand your world—it expands your circle.

So, if you've ever hesitated to travel solo, take this as your sign. The world is out there waiting for you. Not just the landmarks and landscapes—but the version of yourself you'll meet when you step into the unknown with no one to rely on but you. That person is strong, curious, capable, and free.

Let solo travel be your reset, your revelation, your reminder that you are enough all on your own—and also endlessly connected to everyone else who's ever wandered, wondered, and dared to explore.

Chapter 16
Sorcerers of the Falls

Some moments in travel are about distance. Others are about depth. You can cross oceans and borders, or you can stumble into a moment that pulls you further into life than you've ever been. This was one of those moments.

I have always chased the thrill of the unknown, but nothing prepared me for a journey that would feel like both a farewell and a rebirth. My mother had passed away that summer after a battle with cancer, and the grief was the kind that sits heavy in your bones. I didn't just want to get away—I needed to remember there was still beauty worth chasing.

That's when a strange collaboration between my then-husband and boyfriend at the time (yes, life was complicated) turned into an unexpected gift: a trip to Niagara Falls for my birthday.

We took a train through the rolling landscapes of Canada, the kind of scenery that reminds you the world keeps moving even when you feel stuck. Winter had swept through the falls, chasing away the tourist crowds, and for someone like me—someone who loves the quiet—this felt like a blessing. The rushing water roared for us alone.

That first night, we wandered the nearby town and found a haunted house. The place was empty except for us, each creak of the floorboards amplified by the silence. We laughed our way through the darkness, adrenaline mixing with curiosity. It set the tone for what was to come: unexpected, a little surreal, and just on the edge of magic.

The next morning, we stood before the falls, watching water plunge into the depths like liquid thunder. But the real story began in a Starbucks, of all places, where we met a lone barista with a secret. She told us about a man—hidden somewhere nearby—who controlled the colors of Niagara Falls.

Her directions were more like hints, but we followed them anyway, up a dark hill to an unmarked door. When it opened, there he was: the master of the lights. Instead of turning us away, he welcomed us into a room that looked like something between a control center and a magician's workshop.

And then, he let us try.

We pushed buttons and pulled levers, watching the falls shift from emerald green to deep sapphire to fiery crimson. We laughed like children, as if we were painting the night sky itself. For those moments, the grief softened. The world felt bigger again.

Before we left, he handed us certificates—proof that we had, in fact, been the sorcerers of Niagara Falls. I still keep mine, not just as a souvenir, but as a reminder that wonder often waits in the places you don't plan to go.

I could never find that room again. It wasn't a tourist stop, and it shouldn't be. Some experiences are meant to be rare. They live in you precisely because they can't be repeated.

That's the beauty of travel—it's not always about ticking places off a map. Sometimes it's about being open enough to follow a stranger's tip, climb the hill you weren't planning to, and knock on a door you're not sure will open. It's about letting the unexpected pull you back into life.

Niagara was breathtaking, but it wasn't just about the falls. That trip reminded me that adventure isn't always tied to borders or countries— it can also be found in places that touch you in unexpected ways. For me, one of those places became the ocean. My traveling spirit kept pulling me toward it again and again, until I realized it was no longer just scenery—it was part of who I am. The ocean taught me presence, depth, and calm in ways no city or landmark ever could.

Chapter 17
Breathing Underwater

Perhaps scuba diving isn't about visiting a "country" in the traditional sense, but it is a place on this planet—its own vast and living realm. In many ways, it was my traveling spirit that led me here. The same curiosity that carried me across continents eventually turned my gaze downward, to the world beneath the surface. That's where I discovered my love for the ocean—not from a single trip, but from the restless desire to keep exploring, to see every corner of the Earth, even the ones hidden beneath waves.

That whisper below the surface has always called to me. Scuba diving is more than a hobby—it's my sanctuary. The ocean is where my mind calms, my body moves without strain, and my soul remembers how to expand. My fascination with the underwater world comes from an unquenchable thirst for discovery and a need for the kind of stillness that exists only beneath the waves. Every dive is a blend of adventure and serenity—an escape from the noise of daily life and a journey into mystery.

Sylvia Earle once said, "Every time I slip into the ocean, it's like going home." She's right.

The physical side of diving surprised me at first. Swimming against the gentle pull of the current works muscles you forget you have. The water's resistance strengthens my entire body, improves cardiovascular health, and builds stamina. The ocean even burns energy just keeping you warm—up to 500 to 700 calories an hour—so it's possible to have one of the best workouts of your life without feeling like you're "exercising." And yes, after a dive, I'm always famished.

I still remember my first dive clearly : the weightlessness, the quiet, the way my body moved in harmony with the water . It felt as though my muscles, lungs, and mind had all agreed to cooperate for once. Diving isn't just about swimming; it's about mastering breath, staying buoyant, and gliding effortlessly. Research confirms the benefits—studies show that regular diving can significantly improve cardiovascular fitness and muscular endurance. But no study could explain the smile on my face when I surfaced, salt water in my hair, and the world above temporarily forgotten.

That's part of the magic. Underwater, the noise of life disappears. There are no phones. No notifications. No urgent "to-do" lists competing for my attention. Instead, I'm fully present—watching a school of fish shimmer past like living jewels, noticing the soft sway of coral gardens, following the lazy drift of a turtle. This immersion is its own kind of meditation. The steady rhythm of breathing through a regulator slows my heartbeat and quiets my thoughts.

There's a quote I've always loved: "There's nothing wrong with enjoying looking at the surface of the ocean itself, except that when you finally see what goes on underwater, you realize that you've been missing the whole point of the ocean. Staying on the surface all the time is like going to the circus and staring at the outside of the tent." Dave Barry was right—you can't know the ocean by staying above it.

For me, diving is also spiritual. Submerging into the blue reminds me of my smallness in a vast, ancient world. The ocean's sheer scale, the delicacy of its ecosystems, and its relentless rhythms humble me. Every reef, every creature, is a thread in a fabric older and more complex than anything humans have built. This realization not only deepens my respect for nature—it makes me protective of it.

Chapter 18

One Pack, Four Countries, and the People You Never See Coming

Some trips are just vacations. Others change the way you see yourself.

This journey wasn't about packing a bag—it was about unpacking everything I thought I knew about who I was and what I could handle.

I wasn't boarding this flight for a few cute Instagram shots or to check destinations off a list. I was leaving behind emotional wreckage— walking away from a chapter that had ended painfully and abruptly. For too long, I had ignored my intuition, letting emotions and distractions blur the truth. That detour had taken me somewhere dark, but when I finally woke up, I knew one thing for certain: I couldn't rebuild in the same place where I'd lost myself.

I needed movement. I needed distance. And most of all, I needed to remember the version of me who still believed in possibility.

So, I zipped my bag, grabbed my passport, and set off—not just for new adventures and fresh faces, but to reconnect with the strength that had always been mine. **First Stop: Madrid**

When I told my parents I was going backpacking again, their reaction was exactly what I expected: no surprise at all. They know I can't sit still. To keep things budget-friendly, I asked them to reach out to any family or friends in Europe who might have a couch or spare bed. My stepmom contacted her ex-husband—yes, really. (We're that kind of modern, healthy family.)

It turned out to be an unexpected blessing. I stayed with a warm and welcoming adoptive family I'd never met before but quickly grew fond of. I spent a week with them before heading to Italy.

Of course, no real adventure begins without a hiccup. Mine came before I even left the States. Air Canada quietly rescheduled my early morning flight to an evening departure. That change rerouted me through London instead of Toronto, switching me to British Airways. By the time I finally landed in Madrid, I was jet-lagged, slightly annoyed, and— most inconveniently—without my luggage. My suitcase had apparently decided to follow the original itinerary and was hanging out somewhere in Canada. I spent two extra hours at the Madrid airport trying to track it down. Lesson learned: always put an AirTag in checked bags.

Eventually, I made it to Toledo, where I stayed five lovely days with my adoptive family, bouncing between the historical charm of the town and day trips into Madrid. Then, with my finally recovered suitcase in hand, I set off for my next stop: Rome. That's when the trip took a turn for the unpredictable.

The Bahamas Connection That Changed My Trip

A few months earlier, I'd been scuba diving in the Bahamas with Stuart Cove's Dive Bahamas. On my way to the airport, I shared a taxi with a stranger who struck up a conversation. We swapped travel stories, I gave him my business card, and he told me about an app he thought I'd love.

Fast forward to right before this trip—I reached out to him to ask about it. Not only did he remember me, but he'd just found my card a few days earlier. The app was **Couchsurfing**.

For those who've never heard of it, Couchsurfing is like Airbnb but free. You stay with locals—not for transactions, but for cultural exchange. It's about meeting new people, learning their way of life, and seeing the city through their eyes instead of from behind a hotel window. Of course, it comes with a "proceed with caution" disclaimer—you are, after all, staying in strangers' homes.

I downloaded it instantly. My goal wasn't to save money, though that was a nice bonus—it was to immerse myself in culture.

Rome: Where Plans Begin to Unravel

My first potential host seemed normal enough at first. We talked over WhatsApp and even did a few video calls. He told me he didn't live in Rome but visited every weekend, and that the weekend I'd be there happened to be his birthday. He also invited me to a wedding in Tuscany. Cute, right?

I reshuffled my flights and paid extra fees to align my trip with his availability. But just days before my arrival, he told me he couldn't book the place in Rome. Suddenly, I was scrambling to find last-minute accommodation and ended up with something nearly two hours from the city center.

Still, I tried to stay optimistic. I told him we could still meet up. He asked for my location once I landed, said he was driving from Tuscany, and told me to wait for him. Hours later, he sent me a message telling me to come to central Rome instead—without any clear meeting point. Then came the final message: "Good luck with your vacation." Just like that— gone.

Now I was in Rome, with no plan. That's when I decided to try Couchsurfing's "Hangouts" feature, which matches you with people nearby looking to meet up. Within minutes, my inbox was full.

A Martini and Two New Friends

Hungry and overwhelmed, I chose a random restaurant—Caffè Teichner—and ordered a dirty martini. The server offered to make it bigger, and I didn't hesitate.

As I sipped, I got two messages—one from a younger guy in his twenties, another from a man closer to my age named *Sam* (name changed for privacy). The younger guy invited me for drinks that night, but I didn't have a change of clothes and declined. The next day, he messaged again: "Do you have a change of clothes now?" Touché.

Sam, meanwhile, invited me to a rooftop birthday party for someone I didn't even know—classic Couchsurfing. We clicked instantly, conversation flowing as if we'd known each other for years. Later, I met the younger guy for wine. He was respectful, funny, and unexpectedly sweet. We ended up talking for hours.

The City That Wouldn't Give Me a Plan

The next morning, I had to check out of my place and move again. Sam offered me his couch for the night, but I'd still need to find something else afterward. Rome wasn't giving me stability—but it was giving me stories.

And as I'd soon find out, those stories were just getting started.

Chapter 19

Detours, Lost Phones, and the Kindness of Strangers

Travel, for me, has never been about ticking off countries on a list—it's about connection, curiosity, and those unpredictable twists that throw your plans into the wind and replace them with something better. In the last chapter, I wrote about discovering my love for the ocean through my traveling spirit. But it's not just nature that teaches me this—it's also the people I meet, the moments I can't script, and the truth that even when things get messy, the road somehow provides.

That's where Couchsurfing comes in. For anyone unfamiliar, it's a global hospitality exchange where travelers can stay with locals for free—not in hotels, but in real homes. It's about cultural exchange, generosity, and human connection. I started using it not only because it was budget-friendly, but because it opened doors to people I never would have crossed paths with otherwise. Some encounters are fleeting; others become lifelong friends. And sometimes, they're the reason a chaotic trip turns into a story you'll tell for years.

Rome was one of those stories.

What was meant to be a smooth escape through the Eternal City quickly spiraled into a chain reaction of last-minute scrambles. A Couchsurfer who had agreed to host me canceled suddenly, leaving me without a place to stay. That single cancellation set off a domino effect of expensive, inconvenient choices. I ended up in two separate accommodations, both nearly two hours from the heart of Rome. One of them was a campground so far from my expectations that I took one look and knew I wouldn't be sleeping there.

Getting around was its own adventure. Rome's public transportation is limited by curfews, taxis are costly, and Uber doesn't operate there. Instead, they use an app called Free Now. My first experience was a 70euro ride from the airport—an expensive introduction to the city's logistics.

In the middle of this housing shuffle, I met Sam, a local I'd first encountered at a rooftop birthday party. He had that calm, grounded energy that makes you feel like everything will somehow work out. He sometimes hosted travelers but mostly rented his spare room on Airbnb, and when we met, it was already booked. Still, we exchanged numbers—something told me to keep that connection.

When the next Couchsurfer accepted my request, it turned out to be in Frosinone, a town about an hour outside Rome. Locals may turn their noses up at it, but I found it charming in its own small-town way. My host was respectful, welcoming, and even took me out for gelato. I stayed only one night, though, because the next morning I had a modeling photoshoot scheduled in Rome with a photographer named Nicola.

That's when my trip took another turn. After a few photos, we went to a café so I could change outfits—my entire life packed in a carry-on, backpack, selfie stick, and two phones. By the time we walked to the next location, one phone was gone. My Apple Watch confirmed it: already far away.

Losing a phone while traveling solo is more than an inconvenience—it's a logistical nightmare. My iPhone held my business contacts, notes, and crucial apps. And Apple's legendary security meant I couldn't even log back in without a multi-day recovery process. I had forgotten my iCloud password (because of course I did), and without another Apple device, I was stuck waiting three to five days to reset it.

My backup Android kept me somewhat connected, but most of my work lived on the stolen device. Thankfully, it was insured, but the replacement process through AIG had its own complications. They could deliver the new phone to Rome, but not to Morocco—my next destination. International shipping from AIG was slow, and Moroccan customs had a reputation for holding electronics for weeks.

I reached out to Sam, and he offered to receive the phone for me. The plan was simple: if it arrived after I left, he'd forward it to Morocco. But after remembering the customs risks, we changed the delivery to France, where I'd be visiting friends after Morocco. Crisis, sort of, averted.

Still, I needed an iPhone immediately. That's when a Moroccan Couchsurfer I'd been in contact with mentioned he needed one too. We struck a deal: I'd buy the phone in Italy, use it during my stay in Morocco, and hand it over once he transferred the money. Risky? Sure. But it worked out—he turned out to be one of the kindest people I met on that trip.

Back in Rome, my accommodation shuffle continued. Sam's Airbnb guest had canceled, so he invited me to stay. We clicked naturally. That night, he took me to an outdoor movie in a park where they were showing

The Warriors, and the director, Walter Hill, was there in person. The crowd was a multilingual mix—Italians, Spaniards, Latin Americans—and I felt completely in my element.

Sam became my anchor in Rome. We'd meet for coffee at my favorite spot, Fatti di Farina, where I'd order a perfect caffè shakerato. One night, he invited me to a party in a Roman castle. Outside, antique displays glowed under the lights as people sipped wine. Upstairs, a DJ mixed techno with classical house, and I danced until late.

The next morning was my flight to Morocco—painfully early. Since public transportation doesn't run before sunrise, I booked another expensive taxi. Everything was fine… until I realized I was at the wrong airport. Thankfully, I had given myself a time cushion, and my driver, calm as ever, simply drove me to the right one.

I made my flight—sleep-deprived, running on adrenaline, and oddly satisfied. My Roman adventure hadn't gone according to plan, but the mishaps brought me deeper connections, unforgettable nights, and a reminder of why I travel this way.

Sometimes, the best stories aren't found on the itinerary—they're waiting in the moments you can't plan for.

Chapter 20
Morocco: The Unexpected Home

"The world is a book, and those who do not travel read only one page."
— **Saint Augustine**

If you'd told me a year ago that Morocco might feel like home, I would've laughed mid-flight. Yet the minute I landed, something shifted. I wasn't chasing paperwork or a lease; I was chasing peace— somewhere my restless heart could exhale. I expected adventure. I didn't expect to be tempted to stay.

A month before Spain, while I was still in the U.S., I'd started chatting with a Moroccan Couchsurfer. For privacy, I'll call him Maurice (not his real name). At first, we spoke sporadically—quick calls, a couple of video chats—because honestly, I wasn't thinking much about Morocco. Europe (especially Italy) had my attention. But if you've read the Rome chapters, you know a few hiccups nudged my compass south. Through all of that, Maurice stayed consistent: funny, flirty-but-respectful, genuinely curious. His steadiness made me curious right back.

Back to Couchsurfing, my trusted compass

I did what I always do: posted my trip publicly on Couchsurfing and let the invitations roll in. Maurice's stood out—verified profile, a wall of glowing references, and a bio that said he ran a language center. As a wandering English teacher, I perked up. Those casual calls became regular check-ins. By the time I was boarding my flight, I felt like I already knew him.

And yes—this is the same Maurice from the iPhone side quest. He'd asked me to bring him an iPhone from Italy because there are no official Apple Stores in Morocco. At first, I was like, *Seriously?* But it turned out fine.

Arrival mayhem (of course)

A last-minute flight change meant I couldn't fly straight to Agadir. I landed in Marrakesh and took a long bus ride to what I thought was our meeting point: Inezgane. Surprise—my message never got delivered. I was actually in Agadir. Cue a chaotic round of "send me a video of where you are," and Maurice ended up rescuing me from the Agadir terminal. First time we met in person—and honestly, it felt good.

He drove me to his town, Biougra, and walked me straight into his life: the language center (I'm keeping the real name private), his friends, this care network that made me feel like I'd wandered into a family reunion and accidentally been handed a seat at the head of the table.

The Spanish teacher (and my teacher heart)

I immediately clicked with the Spanish teacher at the center. Morocco doesn't only crave English—Spain is a short strait away, and that influence is real. Omar's Spanish blew me away: clear pronunciation, rich vocabulary, smooth flow. He was like Cervantes with a Moroccan twist. I sat in on a class and co-taught a bit—fielded questions about New York, swapped idioms, and played a quick vocab game that pingponged between Arabic, Spanish, and English. The students were shy for two minutes and then unstoppable. It felt like a tiny sunlit reminder of why I love teaching anywhere on this planet.

About two weeks in, the air shifted. No one said anything, but I felt the soft nudge of *"this has been lovely... and it's been long enough."* Fair. Hosting someone for that long—even someone as charming and culturally dazzling as me—is a lot.

Between the tiny frictions, there were big, beautiful highs. One student invited us to their family farm—animals, fruit trees, plates piled high, and the kind of hospitality that makes you forget every flight delay, every missing item, and every headache. We didn't share a language; we shared a table. That's Morocco.

The car hustle that turned into a social club

Before heading to Marrakesh, I needed wheels. I'd reserved a car online. Easy, right? Morocco said, "Not today." Omar took me to the airport, I waved him off, and the rental company—Wheego—refused my credit card because the numbers weren't *embossed* (they were printed digitally). Who cares? Apparently, they did.

Then the Wheego guy leaned in like a spy and said, "Across the road, you can rent a car without a credit card." So... sure. Underground rental cartel energy. I grabbed cash and met the cash-only guy. We exchanged numbers. I kept the car for a few days. We ended up hanging out. He showed me a club where I promptly ran into the first rental guy. Suddenly, I was part of the cash-car crew at Agadir Airport.

When I told my new rental friend I needed the car for three more days in Marrakesh, he smiled and said, "You get a discount now, Zhara." Cute. We met to sign the new contract—price was higher "because of full coverage." I blinked. "This is fewer days. Where's the discount?" He dodged. I said, "Do I look stupid?" Cue car argument while I was literally driving. He got flustered: "Whatever is fair to you, Zhara."

"Not what's fair to me—you said discount. Be honest."

He got it. We landed on a fair price. When I returned the car, he asked if I was staying longer. I had four more days. "Keep it," he said. "From now on, this will be your price every time you come to Morocco— insurance included." Accidentally negotiated a VIP rate by… yelling in traffic. I'll take it.

The Marrakesh misunderstanding (and the makeup)

Marrakesh gave me one of the best bar crawls of my life—a Moroccan who looked Argentinian (his only Spanish line: *Yo hablo español muy bien ,* which did not help), a German polyglot, a hilarious host, and a tribe of global wanderers who turned into instant family. Live music, rule-free dancing, effortless laughter—*this* is why I travel.

Maurice and I had planned to reconnect in Marrakesh so he could see a side of Morocco that looks more like *me*: nightlife, international crowds, my music, my pace. It didn't go as planned. Something about where I was staying (and the overall vibe) made him uncomfortable. To me, it felt insulting—I had embraced his world wholeheartedly. One night on my terms didn't seem like a lot to ask.

We clashed. Then we talked—really talked. It turned into one of the best post-argument conversations I've ever had with a man: raw, honest, respectful… and yes, kind of hot. We apologized to each other. We had a very sweet makeup. Some cultural confusion lingered, but I'm leaving that where it landed.

I also needed space. Enter a last-minute lifesaver—another Couchsurfer I'll call Ignacio (not his real name). He deserves a trophy. He welcomed me same-day, walked me around without letting me get skinned alive, and—this is important—brought cake. Calm, funny, unbothered by my post-drama energy. If Couchsurfing gave awards, I'd hand him one with a glitter cannon.

Before the Marrakesh chaos, I'd done a day tour to the Atlas Mountains —ironically, where Maurice had gone after visiting his family. We'd talked by phone; he'd sent me a photo of a waterfall. I asked the guide if we could stop there. We did. And guess who was there? Maurice. Total coincidence. We stole a few minutes together. I told the guide I just wanted a little time, and he suggested I walk back to the meeting point so Maurice and I could catch up. It had been days. Those minutes were exactly what I needed.

From tourist to "NY" (kind of)

In Marrakesh, I met a Lithuanian mother-daughter duo (they live in Ireland) who needed to kill time before a train to Rabat. By then, I was basically a local—my juice guy knew me, the café guy called me "NY," and a kid on a bike practiced his English with me daily. I showed the ladies around the square, dodged an over-eager henna artist who started painting before I could say no, and haggled their price down from 900 to

300 dirhams. "If I had money," I told them, "I'd be in a five-star resort, not negotiating in the medina." We laughed. One needed a restroom, so I offered mine. Quick stop, quick goodbye, and I hailed them a cab. Tour-guide mode: complete. **Hashish, hammams, and unexpected sleep**

Back home, weed makes me spiral. In Morocco, someone offered me hashish. I said no... then thought, *What the heck?* Different pace, different place. I tried it. Game changer. It felt gentler—more *calm* than *chaos*. Solo, safe, with a quiet room and a glass of contraband-feeling Moroccan wine, I slept like a baby. I'm not a smoker; I'm just into homemade Moroccan melatonin now. **The cousin who made it feel like home**

Maurice introduced me to his cousin—I'll call him Youssef. If consistency were a person, it would be him. Every time we were in Agadir (his turf), Maurice would ping him. Youssef became our unofficial tour buddy and the MVP of hospitality by the end. He even showed up the night before I left just to say goodbye. His English was limited (third language), my French was aggressively duct-taped, and yet we still joked—with charades, sound effects, and pure goodwill. Effort connects people. He helped Morocco feel like home.

Driving into the riad like a maniac

GPS lost its mind and sent me through alleys the width of a diet breadstick—motorbikes, goats, people who absolutely did not care there was a car behind them. I rolled down the window and told the first competent-looking guy, "100 dirhams if you get me out of here alive." He accepted. We made it just in time; cars are banned there after a certain hour. "Are we even allowed to drive here?" I asked. "Yeah," he said. "Just go slowly." I was crawling. Somehow, I made it. Apparently, I can drive in Marrakesh, which qualifies me for Formula 1—or at least bumper cars.

Leaving, but not letting go

All along, Maurice and I tossed around ideas— businesses, language centers, things we might build. Travelers collect pitches like stamps; some are real, some are glitter. Even before I left the States, I was hunting for a place not just to visit but to live. Morocco kept calling. I felt cared for, welcomed—even when I bumped into walls that weren't mine. I wouldn't live in Biougra, but nearby? Somewhere more open, more international? Somewhere I can dance without a committee and enjoy a glass of wine without sparking a town meeting? Maybe.

At passport control on my way out, the officer asked the usual questions and then, casually: "What's your Instagram?" My travel blog is public, so why not? A few hours later—boom—DMs from border control.

Even airport security isn't immune to Couchsurfing energy.

I left knowing I wasn't just leaving a place—I was leaving a feeling. Morocco challenged me, fed me, welcomed me, and rearranged me. And Maurice? I can't label what he became. Not simple, not casual, not easily defined. But important. He's woven through the laughter, the tension, the missed messages, and the soft goodbyes. Not everything needs a title to matter.

I'll miss Morocco. And whether I live there or not, some part of me will always feel connected to it.

Chapter 21
Beyond Borders, Beyond Belief

Travel is fatal to prejudice, bigotry, and narrow-mindedness."
— **Mark Twain**

Traveling abroad is not just about seeing new places — it's about opening your mind, challenging your beliefs, and learning what truly matters. Every trip has taught me that the real journey is inward, shaped by the people we meet, the cultures we experience, and the lessons we carry home.

For me, traveling is freedom. Freedom from routine, from narrow thinking, from preconceived notions. It's about stepping into the unknown with curiosity, humility, and an open heart. When I travel, I don't just collect photos or souvenirs — I collect moments and stories that change how I see the world.

People love to draw lines: right or wrong, black or white, permissible or shameful. But the more I travel — and live — I've learned those lines are almost always drawn in pencil. Easily erased. Quickly redrawn.

In Morocco, I remember watching women gracefully glide through the souks in their long, flowing djellabas. Everything about their appearance reflected curated modesty. In some towns like Biougra, drinking was unthinkable. When I first mentioned wine to someone there, I got a look like I'd said something obscene.

But then, I drove into Marrakesh, and the atmosphere shifted. Rooftop bars buzzed, tourists in crop tops danced to live Berber beats, and conversations flowed freely — with cocktails in hand. The same country, two completely different moral realities.

So which version is right? Biougra or Marrakesh?

Now let's address one of Morocco's more… quirky contradictions: the law around unmarried couples sharing a room. If you're a Moroccan national, you technically can't stay with your partner unless you've got paperwork proving you're married. It's based on Article 490 of the Moroccan Penal Code, which criminalizes sex outside of marriage.

Here's where things get spicy: if you're a foreigner, no one seems to care.

It's like the moral police turn into Airbnb concierges. Two Europeans? Welcome. One Moroccan and one foreigner? Hmm, depends. Two Moroccans? Forget it. Might as well be on the FBI watchlist.

You start to notice the double standard real quick. A Western couple walks into a riad — smiles, mint tea, no questions asked. A Moroccan couple? Suddenly, it's a full-on paperwork parade. What's wild is that enforcement isn't even consistent. Some places ask for marriage certificates. Others don't care. Some hosts frown. Others shrug. It's less "rule of law" and more "vibe check."

And it's not just the law — it's social expectation, especially in more traditional towns. The judgment doesn't always come from police or landlords — it comes from that one auntie across the street with binoculars and moral outrage.

It really makes you question: what's "right" here? Is it the letter of the law, the mood of the city, or the gossip potential of your neighbors?

In the end, you learn to tread lightly. What's fine in Marrakesh might raise eyebrows in Tafraout. You adapt. You respect. And sometimes, you just quietly roll your eyes and move on — because when it comes to travel, understanding a culture doesn't mean always agreeing with it.

Back in Biougra, someone said to me, "Drinking is haram, forbidden." But I couldn't help thinking... forbidden for whom? I wasn't shot gunning beers or stumbling in public. I was sipping a glass of wine — something that, in Italy, is considered a refined part of dinner. In France, it's a love language. Wine isn't the enemy — ignorance is.

If you lack education and moderation, anything becomes dangerous: alcohol, religion, even love.

That's the problem: not the action itself, but the intention and the context.

I moved to Dubai on a whim. I had $10,000, two suitcases, and not a single job offer. No plan, no safety net. Just the feeling that I had to go. Dubai was a masterclass in extremes: glamour and grit, opportunity and exploitation, freedom and restriction. It made Morocco feel simple by comparison.

In Sharjah, where I stayed temporarily, I felt like I'd been dropped into another century. Rules were strict, and even the clothes I wore drew stares. I wasn't happy there, so I searched relentlessly for a job. I walked all day under the brutal sun, handing out résumés to hotels, schools, and offices. Eventually, I found work — but it was in Ajman, another emirate 50 minutes away.

I said yes anyway. Because when you're running out of time, even a long commute feels like a rescue boat.

I had to learn that in Dubai, there's no such thing as a free system. Everything has a price tag — even your own identity.

To rent an apartment, I needed to give 12 post-dated checks — one for each month. To get a car, I had to find someone who'd trust me enough to let me pay later. To drive legally, I needed an Emirates ID. And without that ID, I couldn't do anything: no job, no lease, no phone, no bank account. It was like being a ghost in a luxury mall.

But the moment I had all three — job, car, and apartment — I felt like I had scaled Everest. All within 30 days.

My first teaching job in Ajman turned out to be full of red flags. They gave me a visa, yes, but under a different job title to speed up the process. They also held my passport illegally and withheld part of my final wages. I filed a complaint with the Labor Ministry — and nothing happened. You learn quickly that if you don't have money, power, or wasta (connections), you're disposable.

When I got a better job closer to my apartment in Dubai, I thought I was finally winning. But three months later, they laid me off without notice. No reason, no severance. Just a call from HR and a goodbye.

In the UAE, during your probation period, they don't even have to explain why they let you go.

Once I had my license and car, I learned another fun fact: in the UAE, you don't get pulled over for speeding — you get photographed. A text message arrives with your plate number and a fine amount. I remember getting my first ticket and panicking. But then I waited and the fine was discounted. Apparently, if you wait long enough, some fines get reduced.

Funny how morality and money dance together everywhere.

People often ask me what I believe in. I'm not religious. But I am spiritual. I believe in energy, integrity, and reciprocity. I've seen so-called "holy" people act with cruelty, and irreligious folks show up with unconditional generosity.

I've prayed in mosques, shared iftar with Muslims, sipped wine with Italians, and danced barefoot at temples. My faith is this: live with intention.

I don't care if you drink, pray, or dance in the street. If you do it with grace and purpose, that's enough for me.

Visiting places like Morocco and living in places like Dubai forced me to see how morality shifts with borders. What's shameful in one town is sacred in another. What's criminal in one country is casual in another.

So instead of asking, "Is this right?"

Ask: "Is this right for me, right now, in this place?"

That's the real question. And if we all asked it more often, the world might be a lot less judgmental.

Teaching English in China introduced me to people who invited me into their lives without hesitation — showing that generosity knows no borders.

Driving solo across Moroccan landscapes taught me to embrace solitude and the beauty of my own company.

Joining strangers in celebrations far from home revealed how shared human experiences can unite us beyond differences.

These moments shaped my understanding that being open and respectful allows us to see beyond "otherness" and recognize shared humanity.

As you travel — or simply navigate life — I invite you to ask yourself:

- What do I truly believe about people and cultures?
- Can I release judgment and open myself to learn instead?
- How can I carry kindness and good faith into every interaction?

There is no one "right" way to be. There is only being authentic, compassionate, and willing to grow.

Travel has taught me that the greatest adventure is not in the places we visit, but in the transformation we experience. It's a lifelong journey toward empathy, understanding, and connection — values that enrich every corner of the world.

So whether you're stepping onto a plane for the first time or simply meeting someone from a different background, remember: travel is an invitation to see the world through new eyes, and to become a better version of yourself.

Fear is temporary. Judgment is limiting. Openness is liberating.

Chapter 22
Lost in France, Found in Laughter

"If we were meant to stay in one place, we'd have roots instead of feet."
– Rachel Wolchin

So here we are. I left Morocco with an unexpected hunger to move there. To be honest, I fell in love with the pace. People there work, yes, but they live. I've been exhausted by the constant stress and bureaucracy of the U.S. educational system—my so-called "home." I'm a free spirit. I can't lie, I can't be political. I just do what I love and love enjoying my life. But back home, you become a slave to bureaucracy, cultural ignorance, and the most boring routines ever invented (seriously, who approved that Monday morning meeting agenda?).

So, leaving Morocco left me thinking. But we'll come back to that.

Bonjour, Moissac! Wait... Why Moissac?

My next stop: Moissac, France. Now, you may ask: Why Moissac? Well, it turned out to be a quiet village in the middle of nowhere. Like, really nowhere. The kind of place you'd only go if you knew someone who lived there. Which is exactly my case.

I travel the way some people thrift shop: I know the general vibe I'm going for, but I have no idea where I'll end up. It can be overwhelming. At a certain point, you just need a break. And that's why I decided to visit my lovely friends, whom I originally met while living in Dubai. They didn't move to France permanently, but they have a second home there with their kids.

She was my TOEFL student back in Dubai, and we became great friends. I had visited them a few months earlier in the UAE (that's another juicy story). So what better break than staying with friends in the comfort of a family home with people I love? At least for a few days before my next trip to Italy.

The Great Moissac Travel Fiasco

I arrived in Bordeaux, the wine capital of France—sounds glamorous, right? Except that the welcome was a disaster. Hiccups follow me everywhere. Honestly, I might be cursed. But I can't handle a boring trip. The silliness of typical tourism isn't for me. I need to be part of the local life, and that comes with unexpected chaos.

Getting to Moissac? A pain in the derrière. The only reason I even knew it existed was because of my friends. Otherwise, Moissac? Never heard of her.

I booked my transport through SNCF Connect, aiming to get from Bordeaux Airport to St. Jean train station, then onward to Moissac. My friend said Bordeaux was about three hours away from Moissac. I figured I could do that. Spoiler: it went south fast.

I landed in Bordeaux, found the shuttle to Gare Saint-Jean, and thought, Cool, I got this. I waited for my train with confidence… until five minutes before departure, when I realized I was standing at the wrong platform.

Or was it the wrong hall? Hall 2? Where's that? I asked someone in French if the train was going to Langon. "Non."

Cue panic. A kind staffer told me I needed to take a bus to Langon first, then switch to a train to Moissac. What?! I checked my ticket, and yep— he was right. My mistake? Assuming French transportation makes sense. Bless my optimism.

So, I hopped on the bus to Langon. Smooth? Not really. The bus dropped us all off, and everyone lined up for a second bus. I was like:

Am I the only one taking the train? Nope. Turns out I was trying to board the wrong bus. When they scanned my ticket and said I had to take a train instead, I had to retrieve my luggage from the very back. Tetris, but stressful.

A nice Frenchman helped me dig it out. Merci, kind stranger.

Then came my guardian angel: a lady who spoke Spanish. Finally, a language in which I could express my frustration. I asked where the train station was, and she helped me. Then she asked if I could buy her a ticket and she'd give me cash. Lady, I'd love to, but first I have to not miss my train.

Well… I missed my train.

Sick, Stranded, and Existential

The station? Dead. No cashiers, no stores. Just two vending machines filled with lukewarm drinks (a crime against refreshment).

111

I was sick: congested, exhausted , and sad about leaving Morocco .
Nostalgic. Aware that all those moments were a temporary fantasy. Such
is the life of a nomad—you meet people, build connections, and then
realize it's all fleeting.

Ironically, the one person texting me during all this? The immigration
officer from Morocco. Meanwhile, the Moroccan couchsurfer? Ghosted.
Classic.

This is what happens when you travel. Don't get attached—not to people,
not to places. They're all just passing through.

I wished I had a partner who shared this nomadic life. But as the saying
goes, better to be alone than with the wrong company.

The Moissac Meltdown

There was only one option left: take the next train to Agen, then figure
out how to get to Moissac from there. Easy? No. Trains to Moissac were
done for the day.

At the station, I helped another stranger buy her ticket. She gave me more
cash than it cost and insisted I keep the change. I refused, she insisted
again. I awkwardly accepted. Thank you for funding my future
emergency croissant, mysterious stranger.

From there, it was chaos: no Ubers, sketchy taxis charging 200 euros, and
me crying from exhaustion in Agen station until they kicked me out
because they were closing. Eventually, I bargained a taxi down to 160
euros. Outrageous, but at that point, my soul was already broken.

Finally, I arrived at my friends' second home in Moissac. They greeted me with warm hugs and soft lighting. I nearly collapsed in their arms like a telenovela character—but the nightmare wasn't over.

The iPhone Fiasco: Part Deux

Yes, the cursed iPhone saga continued. SIM-locked again. Apple, Google Fi, AIG, T-Mobile—everyone blaming each other. After two weeks of back-and-forth chaos, I finally got it unlocked. But by then, I was already back in Madrid.

Finally: Family, BBQ & Vineyard Dreams

"Life begins at the end of your comfort zone." – Neale Donald Walsch

The next day was the nanny's birthday. Neighbors came, BBQ smoke filled the air, kids splashed in the pool, and laughter echoed. I felt cared for.

I met the neighbors my friends had raved about—a warm, funny couple who didn't speak English but radiated kindness. Sometimes, words aren't necessary when the vibes are good.

On my last day, they gave us a tour of their garden: vegetables, fruit trees, fresh herbs, homemade honey. It was straight out of a postcard. Life can be simple and beautiful when you grow your own food and live in rhythm with nature.

Before leaving, we visited Lauzerte, a medieval village, and finally Château Lagrézette, a vineyard built around a 15th-century castle. Wine there wasn't just a drink—it was art, culture, patience, and taste all bottled together. **Final Reflections**

What did I learn? Never trust rural French timetables. Don't rely on Uber after sunset. SIM locks are evil. You'll cry, curse, spiral—but eventually, you'll laugh.

Sometimes kindness speaks no language, but you'll understand it anyway. The South of France will heal your heart and fatten you up with BBQ and honey. And wine? Wine is more than alcohol—it's art you can drink.

Chapter 23
When Temporary Feels Too Real

"A friend may be waiting behind a stranger's face." – Maya Angelou

Leaving with More Than Sand in Your Shoes

I left Morocco with more than spices tucked away in my backpack and sand stuck in my shoes. I left with emotions that had no clear home to rest in—a connection that felt deep, conversations that had seemed unforgettable, and then suddenly… silence. That's when you realize travel isn't always just sunsets and laughter. Sometimes it leaves behind nostalgia with a bitter edge.

People you meet on the road almost always pass through your life like a train at full speed. They talk about dreams, plans, and futures that sound like you'll somehow share them. And then—once you part ways—it's as though none of it ever existed. Like it was just a dream you woke up from too soon.

The Illusion of Instant Intimacy

Travel accelerates closeness. You meet strangers in hostels, cafés, Couchsurfing homes, or late-night train stations, and within hours you're laughing like old friends. Sometimes that intensity convinces you this bond will last. But the truth? Most of these people vanish just as quickly as they appeared.

I saw this firsthand in China. I lived in a small city where I was the only foreigner for miles, yet the warmth I received was overwhelming. Strangers offered me food, my students shared their deepest hopes, and once, a woman I met on a weekend trip invited me—without hesitation—to her sister's wedding. That kind of generosity, boundless and immediate, stays with you forever. But permanence? No. When I left China, those beloved faces became memories locked in photos, fading slowly like mist.

The Ones Who Stay

Of course, not everyone disappears. Some people become anchors.

In Dubai, I found rare kindred spirits. One of them, my so-called "guru," was a soul so grounded, kind, and genuine that even years later, our friendship remains steady. Another friend left Dubai for Denmark with her family, and yet we still keep in touch. A third, from France, opened her home to me again when I circled back to Europe. These friendships are proof that sometimes, the road gives you something lasting.

The Letdown After the High

And then, there are the others. The ones you laugh with until your cheeks ache, the ones whose company feels like sunshine—until you leave. Then it's silence. No calls. No messages. Just echoes of something that felt real but wasn't built to last.

That's the hard part about solo travel: the highs are dizzying, but the lows can be crushing. The thrill of new bonds is often followed by long stretches of solitude. And in that quiet, you start to feel the sting of what's missing—a consistent partner in crime, someone to share not just the adventures but also the ordinary in-betweens.

The Ghosting Game

Couchsurfing has given me some of my best and most bittersweet lessons about this. You connect online, swap stories, maybe even hop on a video call. You share hopes, make plans, dream up a little world together. Then the trip ends. The bubble bursts. Suddenly, no more calls, no more messages. Just a silence that feels louder than it should.

It's almost like an unspoken pact: "That was fun. Now it's over." And sometimes, I wish it wasn't. I've always been someone who values lasting connections. But not everyone is built the same. Some prefer their friendships like postcards—beautiful, brief, and left behind.

Am I the Problem?

I've asked myself this more than once. Am I too emotional? Too attached? Too quick to hope for more? Maybe. But I don't think it's wrong to want deeper ties —to see someone and think, *we could really build something.* The reality is, many people don't want that. They're happy with temporary sparks that fade as quickly as they appear.

Lessons in Letting Go (and Keeping What Matters)

Travel forces you to confront the weight of attachment. You learn that not everyone can carry that kind of baggage—and not everyone is supposed to. Some people walk with you for a few steps, and that's all. Others stay long enough to shape you, to leave a mark that lasts years.

The secret is knowing when to release your grip. Laugh when it's time, cry when it hurts, and let go when they leave. Because not everyone is meant to board your next flight. And when someone *does* stay, when a friendship proves itself rare and real, you hold on with both hands.

Final Thoughts

So am I searching for fleeting companionship or hoping for permanence? The truth is, I want both. I want to embrace the joy of temporary connections while still leaving space for the ones that endure. Because both matter. Both teach. Both shape the journey.

Travel keeps reminding me: some people are passing through, and some are meant to stay. The beauty is in being open to both.

"One of the great things about travel is that you find out how many good, kind people there are." – **Edith Wharton**

Chapter 24
Lost and Found in Madrid

"Travel is never a matter of money but of courage." — Paulo Coelho

Madrid Did Not Hand Me Ease

Madrid did not hand me ease. It handed me curveballs: Couchsurfing maybes, hostel heatwaves, and the kind of detours that make you ask, out loud, "How did I end up here?" If you've traveled solo, you know the truth—sometimes it's sunsets, and sometimes it's survival mode.

Italy Round Two: Chasing a Feeling That Wasn't There

Before Spain, I looped back through Italy, trying to catch the spark from my first time there. Lightning, it turns out, doesn't always strike twice.

"The journey, not the arrival, matters."— T.S. Eliot

There was one bright constant: Sam, my Roman lifesaver. I booked a couple of nights in an Airbnb because I had trust issues after the last hosting fiasco, but I still tried Couchsurfing. The host confirmed—then bailed on the first two days. Sam stepped in again. He folded me into his circle, and in four days, I re-met people from my last visit like no time had passed. He even dropped me at the station for my flight run. "One's destination is never a place, but a new way of seeing things." — Henry Miller

Rome's transport turns into a pumpkin at midnight. My flight was at 6 a.m., the last train to Fiumicino left at 11 p.m., so I camped at the airport for seven or eight glamorous hours. Somewhere in that fluorescent purgatory, the Moroccan Couchsurfer called—the same one who'd faded to silence. I didn't shut him down. I liked him. I missed the connection. I also knew it was a summer story, not a forever one.

"Travel isn't always pretty... it should change you."
— Anthony Bourdain

Madrid: My Language, No Plan

Landing in Madrid felt like a breath; Spanish is my home base. But I had no solid plan—just a backup bed because my next Couchsurfing option was throwing red flags (wouldn't take a call, weirdly inconsistent). I'm done playing homelessness roulette.

"A good traveler has no fixed plans and is not intent on arriving."
— Lao Tzu

I checked into **Hostel MYD La Latina**. First room: seven beds, no AC. After I complained: a twelve-bed dorm with AC and zero privacy. No place for the suitcase, lockers every time I needed toothpaste—hostel choreography I'm not built for. When Ramón, a Madrileño I'd just met, offered his couch for my last night, I took it. No AC there either, but at least it wasn't twelve strangers breathing in unison.

"Life begins at the end of your comfort zone." — Neale Donald Walsch

Hangouts, Tinder, and the Near-Misses

Couchsurfing Hangouts can spin a lonely morning into a full itinerary by noon. I was sleep-deprived from the airport campout and couldn't check in yet, but I went out anyway. I even downloaded Tinder (I know). A friend met her husband there, so I promised myself I'd use it for friendship first, not speed dates. One match—a sweet guy—invited me for drinks the next day. He lived four hours away by the beach. Tempting, but I wasn't about to spend more money or send mixed signals. We kept it cordial and moved on. "People don't take trips, trips take people." — John Steinbeck

Another Hangout landed me in a café with a local while I battled T Mobile for the latest round of the phone-unlock saga (a month of drama). He leaned in for a goodbye kiss; I pivoted. Not everything is a rom -com. Platonic is a full sentence.

NakedSpa: Hammam Below, Wild Upstairs

Then a Bolivian guy messaged: "Want to see a liberal club?" Enter **NakedSpa**. The first floor was all hammam—sauna, pool, jacuzzi, towels or nothing. Cocktails were €12 (calm down, Madrid). Upstairs? A fully consenting circus: swings, open rooms, bodies moving without shame. We stayed observers by choice. Entry was **€20**, including flip flops, a towel, and a beer or soda.

"Adventure is worthwhile." — Aesop

At the end of the night, in the unisex locker room, a woman paced topless, furious about her missing shirt. I don't know if she found it or just invented a new trend on the walk home. Also, a couple offered to "accompany" me to the second floor. I declined; they smiled and drifted away. Boundaries respected—in a sex club. File under: Madrid lessons.

From Morocco's ankle -policing to Madrid's shrug at nudity, my sense of "normal" stretched and didn't snap.

Ramón, Casa de Campo, and Caffeine Diplomacy

Real connections found me anyway. Ramón, who was hosting a traveler from India, invited us to **Casa de Campo**. We ate like kings at **Desh**— three full meals and drinks for **€12.50 total** (yes, total). Later, he took us to **Cafelito** in Lavapiés. Spain treats iced coffee like a DIY experiment— espresso plus a glass of ice—but this place had syrups. His guest asked for vanilla; I asked for almond. Hers tasted like dessert; mine tasted like… cold coffee. We suspected both syrups landed in her cup. Ramón, acting as coffee diplomat, got mine remade. Tiny win, big grin.

"Not all those who wander are lost." — J.R.R. Tolkien

His guest later invited me to a rooftop rock concert. I went, checked the vibe, and left early—it wasn't my scene. Ramón and I kept the thread going; we clicked.

Tapas, Tangos, and the Cuban Connector

A Cuban Couchsurfer—tour guide by day, connector by night—swept me to **El Tigre**, where a **€3 drink** comes with tapas large enough to feed a neighbor's cat and then some. Then he pulled me into his weekend event at **Parque del Oeste**: tango, music, a flurry of languages. I went Saturday and then again Sunday, because energy like that is gravity. In a funny twist, Ramón already knew him—and he knew Ramón. Couchsurfing is a small planet.

After the park on Saturday, we landed at a bar, traded stories like old friends at a reunion none of us were invited to, and then… we let it end there. No numbers. No promises. Just the full sweetness of a moment allowed to be temporary.

Last Sleepover, Last City Loop

Before my flight, I ran to **Toledo** to return the carry -on my family had lent me, then spent my last night at Ramón's. No AC (summer Europe, why?), but worth it for the company.

Taxi Closure, Moroccan Edition

My airport taxi driver was Moroccan. Of course, we swapped stories. He howled at my Marrakech Couchsurfing saga, and we traded numbers at the curb. Closure arrives in unexpected accents.

Madrid was messy and human—awkward hostels, odd hangouts, NakedSpa's liberal education, cheap feasts, tango in the park, and friendships that felt instant even when they stayed brief. Not easy. Not curated. But real. And that's why I travel: for the chapters you couldn't script if you tried.

First week in China after moving to Beijing

Khao Chi Chan – Buddha Mountain (Pattaya)

A lovely day at the Berlin Wall with the Rude Bastards Tour of Berlin

A cold morning at the Niagara Falls in Canada

A lovely show in Hangzhou, China

A Fun night with the London Party Pub Crawl

At Dubai 30X30

A Modeling Photoshoot in Rome by Nicola Bonanno

A gathering with new friends in Madrid

Skydiving in New York

Scuba Diving in Cozumel

Scuba Diving in Cozumel

Just random friends in London

Best day with The Rude Bastards in Berlin

Conclusion
The Journey Continues

These travels showed me that home is not a single place on a map, but the courage to keep moving, loving, and learning. Some people stayed. Some drifted away. But every encounter became a part of me. Every friendship, every fleeting connection, every goodbye —all of it shaped me.

The best part is that I have learned as much from those who left as from those who stayed. Loyal friends remain in my life, but even those who were only passing through left lessons behind. That is the beauty of this search —my search for life, in life, and through life. And above all, my search for love.

Yes, I am a hopeless romantic —and I proudly say that. Love is everywhere if you are willing to feel it. Travel sharpens that sense; it teaches you to pay attention, to recognize when something true stands before you. Without these experiences, without heartbreak and serendipity, how would we ever know the real thing when it finally knocks on our door?

That is what comes next. This book closes one chapter of my story, but the journey continues. My next adventure isn't only about places —it's about people, about the lessons of love and dating across cultures, about being married three times and still believing in the possibility of true connection. Because I believe the greatest adventure of all is love — messy, daring, unpredictable love.

I hope these stories have stirred something in you —that restless, hungry part of your spirit craving adventure and freedom. I hope you felt that spark, the one you get when you stand at the top of a mountain, breathless, not because of what's outside you but because of the peace you've uncovered within. Happiness feels too small a word for that joy — it is eternal, expansive, and infinite.

And so the journey continues —not just mine, but yours too. May you keep searching, keep loving, and keep opening your wings without hesitation. The greatest adventures, after all, are always ahead.

About the Author

Zhara Michelle York is a traveler, entrepreneur, educator, and storyteller whose life is defined by bold moves and untamed curiosity. She has wandered through places both simple and grand — from hidden corners to dazzling skylines — always searching for the lessons hidden in the unknown.

For over fifteen years, Zhara has also worked as an educator in diverse settings, teaching everyone from young children to college students. These years in classrooms across different communities deepened her love for connecting with people, sharing knowledge, and inspiring growth.

Her blog, Little Wild Experiences, blossomed into a global community of readers drawn to her raw honesty, humor, and unfiltered storytelling. Outside of writing, she has built a multifaceted career: a Financial Planner with ILN, a Real Estate Consultant with Fathom Realty, and the Founder & CEO of BizNet, a real estate networking platform that merges technology, education, and community.

Her ventures in real estate, finance, business innovation, and education all reflect the same spirit of exploration that fuels her travels — always seeking new ways to create freedom and opportunity.

The Traveler's Guide to Life is the first volume in her memoir series, with future books exploring lessons learned from love, resilience, and transformation. Shaped by countless encounters and defining moments, Zhara writes with a voice unafraid to share the truths most hide.

She believes that by telling our stories — the messy, the magical, and the in-between — we give others permission to live more fully, laugh louder, and love without apology. You can follow her adventures on her blog Little Wild Experiences and on Instagram @littlewildexperiences.